Managed Services Operations Manual

Standard Operating Procedures for Computer Consultants and Managed Service Providers

Volume Four: Support and Service Delivery

SOPs for Client Relationships, Service Delivery, Scheduled Maintenance, and All About Backups

Karl W. Palachuk

Published by

G L B

Great Little Book Publishing

Sacramento, CA
www.GreatLittleBook.com

Great Little Book Publishing

Sacramento, CA

Managed Services Operations Manual: Standard Operating Procedures for Computer Consultants and Managed Service Providers

Volume Four: Support and Service Delivery SOPs for Client Relationships, Service Delivery, Scheduled Maintenance, and All About Backups

Copyright © 2014 by Karl W. Palachuk

Parts of this book are derived from blog posts written by Karl W. Palachuk at http://blog.smallbizthoughts.com.

ISBN 978-0-9905923-5-8 (for this volume)

ISBN 978-1-942115-06-9 (for this volume on Kindle)

ISBN 978-1-942115-02-1 (for this volume on Smashwords)

ISBN 978-0-9905923-1-0 (for the 4-volume set)

ISBN 978-0-9905923-6-5 (for the Kindle 4-volume set)

ISBN 978-0-9905923-7-2 (for the Smashwords 4-volume set)

www.greatlittlebook.com

Electronic Contents

This book includes a few additional downloads what you will find very helpful. These include Word files, and a few other goodies.

If you purchased this book from SMB Books or Great Little Book, you should have received a download link when your purchase was completed.

If you lost that or purchased from Amazon or another reseller, you can register at www.SMBBooks.com.

Please have your purchase receipt ready to register. You'll need the Order ID. If your purchase somewhere other than SMBBooks.com, you'll need to forward proof of purchase to us.

Please respect our copyright and do not make unauthorized copies of these documents.

We welcome your feedback. Please email *karlp@greatlittlebook.com*.

Warning about Used Books

When you register your book online, you agree that the book is no longer returnable for a refund. We simply have to assume that anyone who registers the book is going to download the electronic content and use it. Therefore, the book cannot be returned once the e-version has been downloaded. That also means that the owner of a used copy of the book does not have access to the electronic content. Thank you for your support and understanding.

Managed Services Operations Manual

Standard Operating Procedures for Computer Consultants and Managed Service Providers

Volume Four: Support and Service Delivery

SOPs for Client Relationships, Service Delivery, Scheduled Maintenance, and All About Backups

Karl W. Palachuk

Table of Contents

About The Author

Karl W. Palachuk has been an IT Consultant since 1995 and is one of the pioneers of the managed services business model. One of his books - *Managed Services in a Month* - has been the number one book on managed services on Amazon.com for more than five years.

Karl is a popular blogger among managed service providers and produces a wide variety of educational events each year, ranging from online classes, in-personal seminars, and the only all-online three-day conference in the SMB channel.

"Everything we do," says Karl, "is intended to help technology consultants be better with the business side of their business."

You can always catch up with him at www.SmallBizThoughts.com.

www.facebook.com/karlpalachuk

www.twitter.com/karlpalachuk

www.linkedin.com/in/karlpalachuk

www.pinterest.com/karlpalachuk

YouTube.com/SmallBizThoughts

www.tumblr.com/blog/smallbizthoughts

Acknowledgements

I have written or co-written eleven books before this. With this four-volume set I am publishing my 12th, 13th, 14th, and 15th books. More than any project I've ever been involved in, this set of books has been a HUGE effort and a HUGE collaborative effort.

I have over 100 people to thank for making these books possible. Some are co-workers. Some are friends. Some are business associates. And I am proud to say that some are "strangers." (Not really strangers any more since they helped with this project.)

The Story

The story of this four-volume set has three major chapters. First, I started blogging about SOPs – Standard Operating Procedures – on Fridays. I called it *SOP Friday* and even registered the domain name *SOPFriday.com*. You can still go there to get a list of blog posts in an "index" format.

Second, I put together a big fund-raising campaign at Indiegogo.com to raise money to speed up the publication process. It takes a lot of money to produce a book set like this. As a result, raising money allowed me to speed up how quickly I was able to have the money needed for design, layout, etc.

Third, I gathered up all the SOPs from the blog, plus a number that we've used in the businesses I've run over the last twenty years. I had to reorganize the contents quite a bit to make it make sense. Then I had to fill in some gaps. I was surprised at how much writing still remained. So I got to work at that.

Thanks

Huge thanks go out to my friend Monica Caraway for helping with this project. Monica serves as my Marketing Manager and spearheaded the successful Indiegogo campaign.

And of course I thank every single person who contributed to the Indiegogo campaign. Here are those who agreed to have their names published:

Lars Andersson
Daniel Ashurst
Steven Banks
Scott Bechtold
Sam Berar
Jeff Bolden
Frank Bravata
Sharon Broughton
Lauren Buchland
MIchael Campbell
Brett Chalmers
Jeremy Christensen
Robert C Coop
Ross Coutts
Deal Consulting, Inc.
Ryan Dobb
Jonathan Elliott
Bob Farkas
Randall Garner

David Armstrong
Derik T Bahl
Matt Beardon
Don Bentz
Frank Boecherer
Chris Braham
Rory Breen
Rayanne Buchianico
Dan Buhler
Steve Carter
Stephanie Chandler
Robin Cole
Robert Coppedge
Charles Dalton
Ana Diaz
Benjamin Duncan
Raul Espino
James Forbis
David P Grinder

Thomas H Lem Jr
Jonathan Henderson
Anthony Iaccino
Jamie Jensen
Maggie Jones
Leonard Keao
Jakub Kosiec
Thomas Kragh
David Libby
Joshua D Liberman
Eric Long
Steve Marfisi
Darryl McAllister
Tom McKay
Stanley Ng Kian Meng
Bob Milliken
Simon Morley
Juan Nieves
David Okeefe
Rajendra J Patel
Sheldon Penner
Scott Phillips
Dr Gary Porter
Craig Ray
Adam Rowley
Kenneth Shafter
Dewayne Smith
Vikis Sood
Gjeret Stein
Russ Swall
Thomas Tassi
Don Tibbits

Alan Helbush
Shane Hicks
Raffi Jamgotchian
Candice Jones
Thomas Karakis
Henry Knoop
Louie Kouvelas
Hank Leander

Michael Lindsay
Nick Mancuso
James Martin
Kenneth McDermott
Shane McParland
Bob Michie
Scott Minke
Robert Nelson
Vijay Nyayapati
Manny Oliva
Sheldon Penner
Eric Penney
Duleep Pillai
Marlon N. Ramanan
Alexander Romp
Shawn Scott
Biren Shukla
Ray Smith
Clive Start
Nathan Stone
Rich Szymanski
Sean Thompson
Kevin Tobey

John Vighetto	Kevin Vinitsky
Mark Ward	Josh Weiss
Michael R West	Julian Wilkinson
John Zanazzi	Ron Zayac

. . . And Thank You to the entire SMB consulting community for your continued support over all these years.

    - karlp

Karl W. Palachuk

Section I -

Service Delivery Policies and Procedures

1

The First Client Visit

This is a great topic to kick off the final volume in this four-volume set of books on Managed Services. Everything else precedes this final volume. Here we talk exclusively about delivering Managed Services. Much of the earlier work had to do with running your company, working with client, or even running the service department.

This volume is totally focused *within* the service department on actually delivering technical support. So it makes sense to begin at the beginning: The first time you provide service for a new client.

I know I've said this about a million times, but if you haven't read *The E-Myth Revisited* by Michael Gerber, you should. And if you haven't read it in the last 12 months, you should read it again soon.

One of the hallmarks of a successful company is *consistency.* Think about how franchises and big companies greet you. On the phone, in the lobby, with their signage, and in person: It's always consistent. This is more than simple "branding." It's part of the experience of being their customer. How are you treated when you walk into a Double Tree Hotel, a Starbucks, or a UPS Store? It should be the same everywhere.

Now think . . .

What do your clients experience? Is it consistent? Does the experience promote your goals and vision? In particular, does your first visit set you apart as an expert and a professional, rather than just "a computer guy?" In addition, you want to set expectations for success on this visit and all future visits. You want the client to see that you have Standard Operating Procedures that lead to success for both of you.

I'm not talking about the First Sales Visit here. That's a whole different topic – and should also be standardized. I'm talking here about your first "job" or service visit for a new client.

Pick The Right First Job

When you pick a "first job" you should focus on something that's very manageable. In other words, you want to take on something you can pretty much guarantee to be successful. Install a new PC; fix a virus outbreak; install a firewall; document their network.

Keep a list. Yes, really. Keep a list of "first jobs" that you would most like to have with a new client. Here are the elements of the ideal first job:

1. It is easily defined and agreed upon.

For example, you're going to remove the viruses from _____'s PC and give it a general tune-up.

Here's a very important key to success: You might find all kinds of stuff wrong with that machine. You might find issues with the network (e.g., DHCP is handing out an invalid WINS address. It's not used, but it's just wrong and might slow down network browsing.)

You're not hear to fix everything you find! When you find additional things to fix, make a note and enter a service request.

Even if the additional work is non-billable, don't do it now. For this job, your goal is to get in, do it right, and get out. You want to be very successful, very focused, and very profitable.

2. The job should be small.

PLEASE don't do a network migration as your first job. It's too big and you're a total stranger.

An ideal job can be completed in less than a day. A perfect first job can be completed in 1-2 hours. So now you have a job that's easily defined and easily agreed upon, and it's small. So you can absolutely go in, knock it out, and finish successfully.

The "agreed upon" and "small" components are critical. You want to set expectations, exceed them, and show the client how you operate. You want to find additional work and schedule it for future visits. You want to use your RMM and PSA systems. You want to be 100% professional and set a high standard of success.

Do one thing at a time. Finish it and be done.

3. Do not let them open Pandora's technology box!

What you DO NOT want is to go in for a block of time and see how much work you can get done. Expectations cannot be set in such a situation. No matter how good you are, the client won't get it. You can find a thousand things wrong with a network that the client thinks is just fine. So you end up working for hours and they have no idea what you're doing. You are kicking butt and the client thinks you're plodding along.

Don't do that.

I learned this lesson very early in my career. I needed to set up one new PC. But I got hijacked by a guy who had a brought a PC from home and he couldn't figure out how to get a second hard drive installed (back in the day when we moved pins around). It turns out that was not authorized work. It took time but wasn't billable. And the guy was a doofus.

Now the boss thinks I'm easily distracted and willing to take time off task. Doofus thinks he can interrupt me whenever I come in the door, and fix his stuff on the boss's dime.

There were other similar distractions. At the end of the visit, the boss was all happy. Until he got the bill. "What the hell? You came to set up one PC and I get a bill for four hours?"

This is called Pandora's Technology Box. Some clients never get to see a real technician. So, when one shows up, they think the box is open and they can get all their stuff jammed into one visit. That can never be a successful experience for you or the client. So don't let it happen.

Orchestrate your visit.

4. When you're done, send an invoice for the amount quoted.

Even if you go over the estimated hours, send an invoice for only the amount quoted. This demonstrates that you are a good person and you stand by your word. It also makes a big deposit in the Bank of Good Will. So the first time there's a dispute over fifteen minutes, you've got a history of being fair with the client.

You can see why the job needs to be small and defined. If you give away an extra hour, that's advertising. If you give away five hours, that's unsustainable and unprofitable.

Goals for the "First Job" Policy

I know some of you are thinking that this is "bad" service because I'm not running around trying to get ten hours' worth of work into a two hour visit. But there's a good reason for this policy: You need to establish a pattern of support that is sustainably profitable.

Just as you need standard operating procedures that work every day to make your business run smoothly, you need good client relationships that support your business model. The client needs to learn:

- Each job is clearly defined (and has a clearly defined ending)

- Each job is on a separate service ticket

- You are extremely competent at what you do

- You are honest and reliable. You will do what you promise

- You won't be distracted and taken off task

- When you show up, you're going to work on the items with service tickets. There is no "shoulder tap" tech support here.

- You will use your tools and systems so the client sees 1) that you have them, and 2) that you actually rely on them.

- You will make them happen when you arrive and happier when you leave

I have said on many occasions that clients are like dogs: They will do whatever you train them to do. This includes training by not training. If you train them that they can interrupt you, they will. If you train them that they can add work to a project, they will. If you train them that they can call you in the evening, they will. If you train them that they can make you unprofitable, they will.

They don't do this out of spite or any evil intentions. They're just trying to make their business work the way they want it to. Sometimes that conflicts with what you need to make your business run the way it should.

In your first engagement, you have the opportunity to show the client that you will provide excellent service at a reasonable price, and within your standard operating procedures. This will give them faith to stay inside the process. By that I mean, they'll use the PSA system to create tickets. They won't hound you on email and voice mail. They will treat you as the professional you are, because you expect it and deserve it.

Implementation Notes

Implementing this policy is very easy. It is orchestrated by the service manager, along with the sales department. In many small companies, that's the same person.

Basically, you chat with the new client to create a list of things that need to be done. Then you pick one from your list of preferred "first jobs" and schedule it.

After that, you need to make sure the technician who delivers the experience understands the rules. These are really just rules they should be following already:

- Understand the job as defined in the ticket

- Do not add work to what is in the ticket without permission from your supervisor. Additional work is normally a separate ticket.

- Do not allow yourself to be interrupted

- If you find things that could/should be fixed, but they're outside the ticket, you are NOT authorized to perform that work. Create a new service ticket.

On a first visit, the tech should take extra time to explain "the process" for getting tech support. That means the tech should clearly understand this and be well practiced in it.

There are a hundred ways to start a relationship on the wrong foot. You should define for your company the "ideal" first engagement so you can start off every new relationship on the right foot!

Three Take-Aways from This Chapter:

1. The first support job is also the final hour (or two) of the sales process. The goal is to assure the client that they made the right decision.

2. This policy encompasses a great deal of what makes your SOPs work. The job is well-defined, limited, and designed for success.

3. As you work through the First Job, talk the client through your policies so they see how the big picture operates.

Three Action Steps for Your Company:

1. _____

    _____

2. _____

    _____

3. _____

    _____

2

Guide to A Service Call

There are three stages to any service call. A service call means that a technician goes to a client's office to perform work, as opposed to connecting remotely to client systems. The three stages are pretty obvious: Before the visit, during the visit, and after the visit.

1. Preparation

1.1. Company Materials, Parts, and Tools. Each technician needs to have certain supplies and tools to be able to perform their daily work tasks. In Volume Three (Ch. 21) we talked about the "Scary box" of supplies. You need to make sure that each technician has what is needed to be successful. The goal is to never be onsite without something you should always have on hand.

1.2. Personal preparation. Opinions vary on this, but I haven't changed my tune in 20 years. I believe computer technicians should be dressed professionally. That means a shirt with a collar. No jeans. Decent shoes. You should look like someone who is worth $150/hour if you want to get paid $150/hour. If you look like you work out of your trunk and charge $40/hour, then expect to get paid $40/hour.

1.3. Technical preparation. If you are going to send someone onsite, you should try to have that person work as many tickets as possible while there. There are a lot of little things that can be knocked out much faster in person than over a remote connection – especially with slow machines or slow Internet connections.

Of course technicians should be aware of working in real time (see Volume Three, Chapter Four), working tickets from highest to lowest priority and oldest to newest (see Volume Three, Chapter Seven). But there are important exceptions to these. If a tech is going onsite, he should first look at the service board and print out a list of all open service requests for that client. Then figure out how many he can knock out in the time allotted for the visit. If he can knock out five small tickets in an hour, that can make a big difference.

1.4. Supplies. Think ahead and obtain or arrange to have everything you might need onsite. This includes wireless access to the Internet if the job is to fix or troubleshoot a problem with the Internet connection. It also includes tools and any hardware, software, or supplies that need to be delivered.

2. At the client's Office

2.1. Parking. Please park in Visitor Guest parking as designated. Try not to take spaces close to the building out of courtesy to the clients. Always park in a for-pay parking lot that gives a receipt rather than on street with metered parking. The company pays for all parking fees while on the clock. The company does NOT pay for in and out fees if you choose to go somewhere for lunch other than what is available. The company does not pay for parking tickets.

2.2. Onsite Routine

Follow the Company guidelines for telephone etiquette. In particular, do not use your phone for anything other than to talk to another company technician or third party tech support. That means no texting, no email, no phone calls. This is the client's time.

Follow the Company guidelines for Email Etiquette (See Volume Three, Chapter Twenty-One). Again, unless it's related to solving this client's immediate issues, don't worry about email until you are done with this visit.

Check in with the client contact when you arrive, if possible.

Always work from an SR. If someone has a "new" issue with no service request, create one, get it prioritized, and go on.

Follow the Company procedures for Service Request escalation. If you work on any task for more than the allotted time (60 minutes) you must call another technician or your supervisor. Stop, if you are not making progress, and get another set of eyes.

Remember, at 60 minutes, you must start a TSR Log (See Volume Three, Chapter Thirty).

We have an onsite minimum of 1 hour so:

- Never leave the client's office without checking with the client contact to see if there are other things they need done.

- If they have nothing pressing, then review and work on any open SRs.

- Attempt to put in the remaining time performing some desired and useful work either on the Server(s), workstations, or at a minimum the Network Documentation Binder.

3. After the Visit.

Never be in a hurry to get out of the office.

Before you leave, talk with the Client Contact and convey the status of what you did and all outstanding issues.

Make a final round check with all users especially those who had issues to be resolved.

If required, create Service Requests for all unresolved issues.

At all times, and with every service request you touch, you must keep the PSA up to date. You must work in real time. In addition to keeping the board neat and orderly, this means less clean up at the end of the day. Do not leave the site until the PSA is completely up to date for your visit and all items you touched. This includes:

- Time
- Travel Time
- Mileage
- Expenses (if possible)
- Detailed work documentation including Internal Analysis notes.
- Product delivered to the client. Billable or Not.

Remember: All work must be done on a service ticket. So there is no "shoulder tap" support onsite. If the client wants to add a task, they need to enter a service request. Or the tech needs to create it. But he cannot do the work before the ticket is created. Period. No exceptions. Absolutely.

Comments

Please note that this process brings together many things we have discussed. Obviously, the technician has to know about the PSA procedures, priorities, etiquette, and more.

Following this process consistently has many advantages. It gives the client a reliable, predictable, and positive experience. It keeps the service board clean because the tech is always working in real time. It cleans out a few lower-priority tickets simply because you're onsite.

And to be honest, this process allows technicians with fewer social skills to still connect with the client and provide a personal service.

Three Take-Aways from This Chapter:

1. If you're sending someone to a client's site, make sure they accomplish as much as possible and leave the client feeling happy.

2. There's a lot of common sense here. Train your technicians to pay attention to little things.

3. All work must be performed on a service ticket. If "new" work comes up, create a ticket for it!

Three Action Steps for Your Company:

1. _____

_____

2. _____

_____

3. _____

_____

3

The Network Documentation Binder – NDB

The Network Documentation Binder is exactly what it sounds like. Originally, this was simply something that emerged from the way I ran my consulting business. Then it emerged into the *Network Documentation Workbook*. After that, we literally used that workbook and the forms in it to maintain our clients' networks.

Find out more about the *Network Documentation Workbook* at www.networkdocumentationworkbook.com.

Here's the sad truth about documentation in our industry: It sucks! There are 948,253 different ways to document a network. And 99% of the time, that documentation is either in the head of the technology consultant or in the possession of the technology consultant.

That information belongs to the client. The client should have a copy. The copy at the client office should be up to date. If you're a small shop and you personally die or are incapacitated for some reason, the client needs to be able to hire a competent technician and that person should be able figure out the network VERY quickly based on the documentation.

That almost never happens. I can honestly say that we have seen exactly ONE well-documented network with a new client since I went into consulting fulltime in October of 1995. One.

All the other networks – hundreds of them – had either zero documentation, very poor documentation, or some amount of poor documentation maintained by the owner or onsite IT person.

Here's the most interesting change in the last twenty years: Consultants have gotten better and better at tracking these thing. We have tools. We have resources. We have a PSA and SharePoint and OneNote, and all kinds of cool stuff.

But we haven't been good at making sure the *client* has a copy of all that stuff. Even if you have an awesome system for documentation, you need to make sure that you print it out and give it to the client at least once a year.

Holding Documentation Hostage is NOT Job Security [Rant]

This is one of my absolute pet peeves. I hate the fact that our industry is filled with people who think that they might keep a client because the client doesn't know the passwords, the configurations, the warranty information, etc.

Time and time again, we have acquired new clients who had zero documentation. Many of them could not get the passwords from their old I.T. consultant. The consultants literally refused to give the client access to their own equipment.

This is a favorite rant of mine. Why don't these consultants get sued all the time? How come clients never have their attorney write a letter simply stating that the client has paid all their bills, nothing is in dispute, and the client owns the information stored by the I.T. consultant?

It doesn't have to be a nasty-gram. The letter can be very nice but stern. But it never happens. Ever. Ever.

We have had clients pay us thousands of dollars to crack into their systems and then re-document them rather than face off against their former consultant. This is beyond my comprehension. (It does, however, give me a level of confidence that I won't be in a lawsuit. If they're not going to sue someone like that, they sure as hell won't sue someone who is conscientious.)

Anyway . . . remember the context here. Keeping passwords secret and not giving the client access to their own documentation was not a successful job security strategy for 100% of the "other" I.T. consultants we followed.

When a client has decided to find a new consultant – for whatever reason – the client is about 90% gone. If they no longer want you for their tech support, they will leave. And my experience is that they will pay large sums of money to make that happen. So hoarding some passwords won't do you any good.

One of the reasons I wrote my first book, most of my intervening books, and the this four-book series, is to raise the quality of service provided by technology consultants. Keeping passwords and bullying (former) clients is childish and unprofessional.

The client has paid for the hardware, the software, the installation, the support, the maintenance, and the wires in the wall. They own it. Every bit of it. Unless you have a HaaS agreement (hardware as a service), you own nothing.

That means the passwords belong to the client. The configuration information belongs to the client. The configuration backup files belong to the client.

Be Professional!

What's the most professional way to handle all this? Do the best job you can of documenting the client's systems. But make sure the client gets a copy at least once a year.

In fact, I recommend that you send someone to get a photocopy of the client's documentation binder once a year and put that into the PSA as a PDF document. We also burn the PDF file to a DVD and give it to the client, to be stored with their permanent backups.

When you lose a client, graciously make sure all of their documentation is up to spec. Print it out and update their binder. And then hand it to the owner with a stern warning: Let the new I.T. Consultant use this, but never let them take it out of the building.

We had a client who left us for two years and then came back. They were with us for ten years. One of our people had a disagreement with their new front office manager, and the owner decided to side with her office manager (which is probably the right thing to do).

Anyway, they fired us and hired someone else. We created a service request to make sure all the documentation was up to spec and perfect. After all, if we leave with class and style, we might just get invited back some day.

Just at that time, one of our employees decided to spread his wings and go work for a larger organization. Well, he ended up working for the company that had taken over our client.

When we met up for beers shortly thereafter, he reported that there was *zero* documentation of the site. The new company had removed the network documentation binder and put nothing in its place.

In fact, the new company had a manager who believed that his personal possession of this kind of information gave him power and job security. So no one could touch a router except him. No one could touch Active Directory except him.

It was, in Josh's opinion, a huge step backward. I agreed.

After two years, the client came back to us and we re-created all of their documentation. Plus we made sure they knew that they need to guard and value that documentation as a valuable resource.

The Network Documentation Binder – NDB

[End of Rant]

I went through all that to make the point: Documentation is important. In fact, it is central to what you do. Look at this four-book series. It's all about documenting your processes and procedures. Time and time again we talk about documenting client systems.

Documentation should be the one thing that differentiates you from the competition. What you do. What you see. Everything.

So the Network Documentation Binder – or NDB – evolved out of our standard practice of documenting machines, networks, and configurations. Remember, back in the days of NT 4.0, you needed the drives for everything or you could not load the operating system.

So the Machine Spec Sheet emerged so that we knew which video card was used and could have those drivers ready if something went wrong. And the NIC. And the sound card. And so forth.

Automated systems, such as your remote monitoring tool, give you massive reports with all this data. But the useful 6-10 items of data are hidden among 1,000 other items you do not care about.

In 20+ years managing I.T., I have never found it useful to list every .dll version of every DLL on every computer in an office. But I have found it extremely useful to know the exact video card or network card!

The NDB has these basic components:

- Title Page/Front Cover
- Table of Contents
- Fix-It Request List
- Fix-It List Priorities
- Backup Log
- Notes Sheet
- Network Diagram
- Network Summary Page
- Shared Resources
- Exchange Specifications
- Server Software Summary
- IP Address Allocation
- Hard-Coded IP Addresses
- Router Configuration
- Firewall Configuration
- Machine Specifications
- User Records
- Product Information
- Internet Domain Registration Information
- Backup Procedures
- Monthly Maintenance Checklist
- Password Policy

. . . most of which are discussed in this four-book series.

The NDB is not intended to be 100% of the information about any machine or the network. It IS intended to give you the important and non-obvious information you need to get systems working again when they break.

How do you make that massive network-connected faxer-scanner-printer connect to the server, deliver faxes to the intended recipient's email, and drop scans into the correct directories on the public share? I don't know – but it's in the documentation!

More fundamentally: How many physical drives are in the server? How are the RAID arrays configured? What's the domain administrator password? How is the firewall configured? And what is the backup strategy? (See Section III of this volume.)

The NDB covers the basics of users and desktops because, to be honest, those are simple and mostly-disposable resources. All the important company data are stored on the server and backed up. So if a user leaves the company or a desktop computer crashes, no company-critical data are lost. Still – there's enough information there so that re-building a desktop is as fast as possible.

On the more arcane configurations, the NDB does into more detail. Which publicly-visible ports are forwarded to the server? How do users gain remote access to their desktops? How is the BDR (backup and disaster recovery) device accessed in an emergency?

Implementation

There are two basic approaches to building your NDB. First, you will gather up some information when you take on the client. Remember Chapter One: Your First Client Visit. An ideal first job will touch each computer.

Whether it's installing RMM agents or doing desktop tune-ups, the opportunity to touch every machines means you can start building the machine spec sheets. You'll also need to know the IP addressing of the network, and some information about the server and firewall.

Make it a policy and a norm within your business: Every time you touch a piece of equipment, you document it.

The second approach is to do the documentation all at once. You'll miss a few things because you don't know they exist. But for the most part, you can document most small networks in one or two hours. This is also a good first job. Just hang out in the client's office awhile and get to know people.

When you're done with the documentation, photo-copy or scan everything (whichever is easier and faster for the client) so that you can have someone enter it into your PSA. The client should have a physical Network Documentation Binder that lives next to the server. You should have all of that information as one or more documents in your PSA.

Here are the two easy methods for keeping the NDB up to date:

1) Whenever you make a change and you are onsite, enter the change into the NDB. Sometimes this means updating existing pages. Other times it means that you will create a new page. Just do it.

2) If you are working remotely and make some significant change, take a screen shot or create a PDF document. Then email that document to your in-house contact and ask them to a) Place it in the "c:\!Tech\Tech Notes" directory on the server, and b) Print it out and put it in the NDB.

Each month, when you do monthly maintenance, you will need to add a few notes to the NDB, and maybe straighten it up a bit.

I know it sounds morbid, but the ultimate test of your success is that you could be hit by a bus and your company would still continue to provide perfect service to the client because everyone documented everything they did.

For most clients, the NDB is maybe 25 pages. For some, it starts out as ten. There's one for each server, one for each workstation, maybe three for the network, and one for each major device or line of business application (LOB).

The NDB is never intended to be a 200-300 page document that no one ever reads. Just the opposite. It is the most basic, most fundamental, most important information that a *competent* technician will need to come up to speed very quickly if you and your company are suddenly gone.

Three Take-Aways from This Chapter:

1. Every client has an NDB. Everyone has the job of keeping it up to date.

2. If the building is about to be uninhabitable, the one thing you will need to take with you is the NDB: What goes in it?

3. It's easy to get lazy about keeping the client's version of the NDB up to date. Don't do this. It is very important that they can "check your work" at any time and find it's up to spec.

Three Action Steps for Your Company:

1. _____

_____

2. _____

_____

3. _____

_____

4

How Do Service Requests Get Into Your System?

In the old days of break/fix computer support, "jobs" got into your "system" by any way a client could get your attention. This was generally fine, but a lot of jobs didn't get your attention until they were emergencies. So you spent a lot of time putting out fires.

With modern tools, we have more (and better) ways for requests to get into your system AND you have a system! When I speak, I make the point that your system should be designed so that nothing gets lost, dropped, or forgotten. The most important piece of that process is getting every request or task INTO your system.

Overview

In the days of break/fix, things generally got into your system by one of these methods:

- Phone call

- Client interaction (conversation or shoulder tap)

- Client email

- Technician discovers an issue

We still have all those things, of course. But you need to figure out how they translate into tickets in the system. It is critical that every request or task get into your PSA system. Please review the chapter on *Working In Real Time* (Volume Three, Chapter Four).

I know it can be overwhelming to have hundreds or thousands of tickets and tasks in your system. But this is really good news. It means you know the limits of the workload in front of you. You know how high it is and how wide it is. You know how many hours you expect to get "caught up" on the work. It is good!

In addition to the old, break/fix methods, we'll add a few simple additions:

- Client enters a ticket into the portal
- Client emails a ticket into the system
- Ticket is generated by the RMM (remote monitoring and management) tool
- Ticket is generated by your staff
- Ticket is generated by your back office support team

Create a Flow Chart

On the next page is a simple flow chart that includes some of the methods discussed here. You can easily create your own in Visio (or even PowerPoint). This chart includes the process we will discuss again in Chapter Eight on *Service Ticket Updates*.

Once everyone in your business understands the flow of incoming tickets, then they can be more efficient. And they will understand why you need to push clients to create their own tickets!

When you talk to a client about an issue, the words to use are: "Do you want to enter a service ticket, or shall I?" In other words, offer to do it, but make it clear that it's really their job. You should also be clear that you can't do any work except on a service ticket.

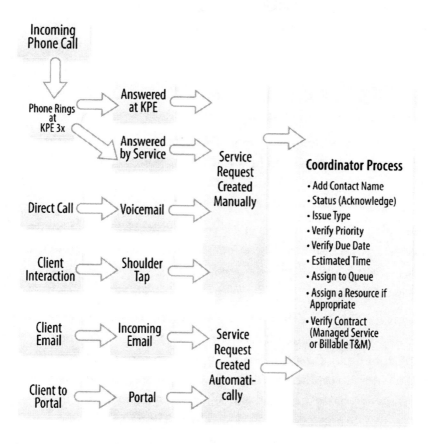

Whether it's billable or covered by a managed service agreement, a ticket is the place where you keep note, track employee time, track the status of the issue, and document when the work is complete. It is the center of what you do on the service delivery side! So ya gotta have a ticket.

For some reason, clients want to pick up the phone and instantly talk to the highest level technician, interrupt whatever that tech is doing, and have their problem solved. That's not the way the world works. That's interrupt-driven break/fix. We sell managed services.

Train your staff to enter tickets in the system. All work must be done from a service ticket. Ideally, the person who answers the phone won't be a technician, so all they can do is enter tickets.

One of the key selling points of a PSA system is that you'll be able to generate reports to tell you how much time you actually spend on each client and each issue. In order to do that, you need a ticket for everything and you need to log time correctly.

Train your clients to use the client service portal or send email to support@yourcompany.com. All PSA systems either accept tickets by email or work with third party applications that convert email to service tickets.

Clients need to know that entering a ticket in the system is the fastest way to get support. First, it creates a ticket, which is the most important requirement to getting support. Second, the PSA system will text or page someone. Either the service manager, the service coordinator, or the person responsible for monitoring the board. Someone will actually get a text message, an email, or both.

Calling, however, can only result in the conversation: "Do you want to enter a service ticket, or shall I?" It is one step prior to creating a ticket.

Implementation Notes

This Standard Operating Procedure is really 50% documentation and 50% implementation. First, you need to document all the ways that tickets get into your system. Then you need to figure out the flow that moves them from the introduction stage to the actual service department. In the diagram example, it is only after the "Coordinator Process" that work can actually be done on a ticket.

After you define your process, you need to train your staff and make sure they all understand that this is how things will flow. Next, you need to train your clients and assure them that the ticketing system is the fastest way to solve their problems.

Finally, you need to enforce this. Don't let technicians work without a ticket. Don't let clients call up and interrupt you.

As you'll see throughout the rest of this book, there's a flow to managing tickets. You caress them you. You massage them. You group them together and manage them. You push them gently through the system. Always moving forward. Always moving in the right direction. The system works because it is a *system*. It's not a disorganized collection of activity motivated by the last request you received.

Three Take-Aways from This Chapter:

1. Document every possible way for tickets to get into your system. Which of these do you *prefer*?

2. Create a preferred process. Then train employees and train clients.

3. Make sure you create a diagram of this flow and use it to train new technicians. Maybe even post it on the wall.

Three Action Steps for Your Company:

1. _____

_____

2. _____

_____

3. _____

_____

5

Response Times - Guarantees and Delivery

One of the key components to building a happy client base is proper management of expectations. Some people think of this as "manipulation" of some kind. But it's not that at all. Every successful company has standard operating procedures. These guide our activities and keep us profitable and moving in the right direction. Where two organizations interact (e.g., you and your client), both sides have a reasonable expectation of what that interaction will look like.

After all, when you receive service, one of the first questions is "When can I expect that to be done?" Part of the appeal of a 30 minute oil change is that you know the time frame without asking.

There are lots of variables here. How do you communicate with clients (PSA portal, voice mail, email, telephone)? How do clients try to communicate with you (Facebook, Twitter, LinkedIn, web form, fax)? Then there's the response times as defined in your service agreement, as defined in your PSA system, and as you've "implied" via your personal communication.

On top of all that you have unspoken assumptions . . . on both your side and the client's. Let's start there.

First: Drop Your Assumptions

The unspoken assumptions of the client and the service provider are the biggest cause of problems. Most of the time this is YOUR fault because 1) You didn't set reasonable expectations; 2) You assume the client wants everything right now; and 3) In any service relationship, the person receiving the money in exchange for service is responsible for managing that relationship.

How do you set reasonable expectations? Well, you can start with a one-sheet handout that describes your priority system (see Chapter Seven, *Setting Job Priorities*) along with a one-paragraph summary of your written response times from your service agreement.

You also set reasonable expectations every time you communicate with a client. You can mention your after-hours policy ("We don't work evenings and weekends."). When a service request comes in you can try to schedule the work for 1-2 days out.

When you answer the phone and enter a new service request, you need to give the client an idea of when you'll be able to work on their issue. Note: It does NOT have to be immediately, within 15 minutes, or within an hour. It can be "this afternoon," tomorrow, or next week.

You are valuable and you schedule your time for maximum efficiency. You prioritize service requests from Highest to Lowest and Oldest to Newest. That's reasonable. Set reasonable expectations.

Now let's look at the mechanics of response times.

Guaranteed Response Time

You need a service agreement. If you don't have one, start with one of my other books, *Service Agreements for SMB Consultants*.

In your Service Agreement, you should state two or three kinds of response times. And don't just let them sit on the paper: Explain them to your clients. You don't want them to think all their problems will be fixed in 60 minutes, no matter what the issue is.

Response Type One: Acknowledgement

This means that you communicate with the client and let them know that you've received their request. This is, strictly speaking, your "Response Time." You have responded and now you can give them a reasonable expectation of when you can start working on the request.

It is very reasonable to promise to acknowledge all service requests within one hour. Depending on your processes, this might be by email, voicemail, or telephone. I don't recommend merely clicking "acknowledged" in your PSA tool. Your client probably doesn't hang out all day on your portal.

Response Type Two: Work Begins

This is what most clients think of as response time, until you educate them. This is when the status moved from "Acknowledged" or "Schedule This" to "In Progress."

You will have different times for different priorities. You might have 1-2 hours for a Priority One ticket; 4 hours for a Priority Two; 24 business hours for P3, and 1 business week for a P4.

You might not have guaranteed times for working on P3 and P4 tickets as you'll want to schedule those anyway. Clients only care about fast response to urgent matters (P1/P2). They are often concerned that P3 and P4 tickets won't ever be resolved, so you need to make sure that's not the case. But you may not need to have guaranteed response.

Response Type Three: Resolution

We never use this. We do not guarantee that issues will be resolved within a specific amount of time. You might try this, but NEVER get yourself in a position of losing money systematically because you over-promised.

Promising a resolution time is not (usually) a reasonable expectation. You want to set reasonable expectations, so don't promise a specific time to resolution unless you have to.

All of these are "Guaranteed" Response Times. That means they're written down in your service agreement and you signed it. That's a promise!

Side Note: They Gotta Use The System

In order for these response times to work, clients must use your system. See the last chapter. That means, the client needs to call your service phone number. Or enter a ticket in the portal. Or sent an email that's turned into a service request.

If clients call a cell phone, that doesn't count. If they talk to a tech in the field, that doesn't count. If they Tweet something on Twitter or post a complaint on Facebook, that doesn't count. If they bitch on Yelp, that doesn't count.

When someone checks voice mail or gets a request in person, they should put in a ticket. But the clock starts when the ticket is entered, NOT when the client goes around your process. Once your team knows there's a problem, you need to enter a ticket and begin working your process. But it is unreasonable for a client to go outside your process and then hold you responsible for your promises.

Actual Response Time

Meanwhile, at your office, you have a tighter process.

It should be your goals to Acknowledge all service requests within one business hour. And if you have an office manager or someone who stays at the office most of the time, they should be able to acknowledge tickets within 15-30 minutes.

Technicians are NOT expected to check voice mails all day long, or to ever receive a service request by cell phone or voice mail.

Technicians are NOT expected to hang out on email all day, or ever receive a service request to their email address. Technicians check email three to five times a day.

Internally, you need to have a process to acknowledge all service requests within one business hour. This is very manageable and reasonable. Just do it.

Service delivery (actually starting to work on an issue) depends on the priority. You need to make sure you have a chart that lists your response times. In my opinion, it's okay to set internal goals that are much stricter than the promises in your service agreement. I think one hour to begin work on a P1, two hours for P2, and eight business hours for P3 is very manageable and reasonable.

If your internal process is always better than your written promises, you'll have no problems keeping your written promises.

Your PSA system will automatically track how long it takes to go through each step of the service delivery process. Too many statistics can be worse than not enough. But you should track time to Acknowledge, Time to Begin Work, and Time to Resolution for each service request. You can then run reports by priority and get additional information about how you're doing.

Special Case: Priority One or Server Down - After Hours

There is one important exception to response times that needs a little attention. Servers almost never go down. But when there's a true emergency that needs immediate attention, you need to have a standard process for that.

Quite simply, your response time should be *As Soon As Possible.*

After hours, on weekends, or on holidays, the response time will be as soon as possible given the resources available. With luck, you have one person assigned to be "on call" for emergencies. This person must never work on non-emergencies outside of business hours.

When a P1 emergency comes up, here's a simple process that works for us:

- Call each person on the client call down list systematically until someone is reached (this list is stored in your PSA system)

- Inform them that there is an issue with their system

- Request directions as to how to proceed. After hours work is always billable, so it must be approved.

- If you reach a voice mail system, leave a message stating that there is a problem and ask how they wish to proceed. Leave the main service phone number/extension.

- Continue calling through the list until you reach someone or exhaust the list.

- Once you reach someone:

  o If after hours work is requested, inform or remind the client of our after-hours rate and then find out when to proceed

  o If after hours work is requested, inform the client that there must be someone from the client's company available to get our technician in and out of the building and office as needed

Note: The client must have a representative with full access present at all times in the office while our technician is onsite.

There are other restrictions for after-hours work. See Volume Three, Chapter Nine and also Chapter Seventeen of this volume.

The Bottom Line: Reasonable Expectations

Never forget that you are running a service business. We get into this business because we want to provide service. But if you don't stay profitable, even during an emergency, then you won't be around to provide service in the future.

The thing about Standard Operating Procedures is that they provide a "normalcy" to what you do every day. You CAN expect problems. You can expect emergencies. You can develop a standard response that keeps the client happy and keeps you from pulling out your hair.

Your job stress will be much lower when you realize that you can schedule work in advance and never run around putting out fires. Many people say they want that, but not everyone is willing to implement processes and procedures to make it happen.

Three Take-Aways from This Chapter:

1. Develop "internal" and client-facing response times that make sense for your business. Document it. Train your employees.

2. Don't let clients bully you into faster response times on low-priority items. You keep your system working smoothly because you prioritize your work!

3. Develop a one-page handout for clients defining priorities and response times.

Three Action Steps for Your Company:

1. _____

   _____

2. _____

   _____

3. _____

   _____

6

Ticket Statuses to Use and When to Use Them

This chapter assumes you have a PSA – professional services automation – system. That means Autotask, ConnectWise, TigerPaw, etc. The goal of these systems is to have one place to automate your business, keep all your critical data in one place, and make you more profitable.

I am often asked whether it makes sense to have a PSA if you're a small shop. One or Two people. The answer for me is YES. You use a PSA to make everything work better, and to keep track of all the things that need to be done in your business. Those functions need to be accomplished without regard to size. The question is, how much do you pay, and is it worth it?

Once you pick a PSA, you need to create "statuses" to keep track of things. "What is the status of that ticket?" means, is it in progress, are you waiting for something, are you on hold, etc.

If you've managed databases, you've had the problem of letting everyone enter whatever they want in a field. Thus, you get

- On hold
- Hold
- held
- Holding
- Hold per Karl
- suspend

- defer
- shelve for now

. . . and that results in a field that's very hard to search on. In fact, there may be various meanings to these phrases that make it more complicated.

With a PSA system, you need a standard set of statuses that everyone agrees to . . . and that you use consistently. There should be a short list of standard statuses. Don't get too bureaucratic and try to create a perfect status for every possible scenario. Assuming the service coordinator massages the service board daily (see Chapter Eleven), then it's okay to have a few oddball tickets that are just waiting on the service manager.

Here's what we do:

Overview

You should have as few statuses as it takes to get the job done. Every status you create will result in a layer of management, however minor. 90% of your tickets will be just a handful of statuses. So you need to focus on making those "categories" as useful as possible.

Your statuses should be as obvious as possible, and should be meaningful to both technicians and clients. For example, "waiting on parts" is easy to understand. "Pending administrative review" is meaningless babble until you define it for someone.

Your statuses need to be consistent with your business.

I talk about the statuses we use because they represent the way we run OUR business. Your business will be different and you need to determine the statuses that will reflect the way you want to do business. If you don't already have a well-established process, then I recommend a Visio diagram of how tickets get into and out of your business. Visualize the flow of service requests through your system and then use that to document your process.

If you have a well-established process, the ticketing system should automate that. If you don't have a process, the system should help you put one in place.

I recommend you start out with just these statuses:

- New
- Acknowledged
- Assigned
- Schedule This (or Ready to Be Worked)
- Scheduled
- In Progress
- Waiting Materials
- Waiting Results
- Waiting Customer
- Waiting Vendor
- On Hold
- Completed
- Closed

If you have a backend or elevated help desk such as Third Tier (www.thirdtier.net), then you would add a few statuses for communicating with them, such as Assign to HD - Approval Needed, Assign to HD - Approved, and Assign to HD - Not Approved. We use this format only so that all the help desk tickets can be sorted together.

Under certain circumstances, you might allow clients to update the status of tickets. We do not allow this for any tickets. When clients create tickets, they are in the "new" status. After that, all status changes are done within our company or by the outsourced help desk.

Status Details

Now let's look a little closer at what each of these statuses mean. I know it is "mostly" obvious, but not completely obvious. Note also that the various roles may be played by just a few people – maybe even just one.

- Status: New

  This is the default status assigned to all new Service Tickets. All tickets should start with this status (and should be in the Client Access queue). This triggers the PSA to send alerts to managers, etc. so we know we have a new ticket.

  Once the ticket is reviewed by the Service Coordinator, an acknowledgement is sent to the client. At this point, the ticket status is changed to Acknowledged.

  No Time Entries can be logged against a ticket in this status.

- Status: Acknowledged

  This status indicates that the service team is aware of the new ticket and it has been assigned:

  o   The appropriate Priority

  o   An estimate of time for completion

o   The appropriate Required Date

o   The Issue Type

o   A technician if appropriate

o   The appropriate queue for further work

(See Chapter Eight on *Service Ticket Updates.*)

When a ticket is set to this status, the PSA system will send an email to the client contact indicated in the ticket, informing them that the status has changed.

The help desk / back office should not change any existing ticket to this status.

No Time Entries can be logged against a ticket in this status.

- Status: Assigned

This status indicates that the ticket has been assigned or re-assigned to a technician.

When a ticket is set to this status, the PSA will send an email to the tech and may optionally send an email to the client contact indicated in the ticket, informing them that the status has changed.

The help desk / back office should not change any existing ticket to this status.

- Status: Schedule This

This status indicates that work for this ticket is ready to be Scheduled or Re-Scheduled. i.e. The parts have arrived, the end user has responded to an email, etc.

When a ticket is set to this status, the PSA will send an email to the Service Manager informing them that the status has changed.

Note: This is the most common status that tells a technician: You can work this ticket. We have the information, we have the parts, we have the approval, it's assigned to the right queue, it's assigned to the right service agreement, etc.

No Time Entries can be logged against a ticket in this status.

- Status: Scheduled

This status indicates that technicians have been scheduled for this ticket.

The help desk / back office should not change any existing ticket to this status.

- Status: In Progress

This status indicates that work is being done on the ticket and progress is being made.

We use this status to literally indicate that someone is working on this ticket right now. If you have five technicians, you would expect to see five tickets with this status.

Internally, this status designates that a ticket is being worked on, and therefore no other techs should work on the ticket. You avoid rework by having only one person work on a ticket at a time!

In a perfect world, you will change a status to "In Progress" when you begin working on it. Having said that, there's no point in slavishly following that procedure if it adds nothing to the smooth working of your department.

- Status: Waiting Materials

The Wait Materials status indicates that work cannot proceed until certain software or hardware is acquired.

- Status: Waiting Results

This status indicates that the service team is waiting on results or output from work performed or changes made. For example, you may have changed a registry entry to fix a problem, and now you are waiting to determine whether you were successful.

- Status: Waiting Customer

This status indicates that the service team is waiting for input, response or work product from the client.

- Status: Waiting Vendor

This status indicates that the service team is waiting for input, response or work product from someone other than the client. i.e., Waiting on ISP or copier tech.

Note on "Waiting" statuses: Don't have too many. But you need a few. After all, you sometimes wait on parts, wait on clients, wait for test results. Begin the statuses with the word "waiting" so that they are all sorted together when you massage the board (future topic).

For all waiting statuses, the following is true:

Within the PSA ticket, the notes section or the most recent Time Entry should contain all relevant notes indicating what you are waited on.

When a ticket is set to this status, the PSA will send an email to the client contact indicated in the ticket informing them that the status has changed.

- Status: On Hold

This status indicates that the Service Manager has called for a hold on any work to this ticket. No one is to perform ANY work on this ticket.

Within the PSA ticket, the notes section or the most recent Time Entry should contain all relevant notes indicating what you are waited on.

When a ticket is set to this status, the PSA will send an email to the client contact indicated in the ticket informing them that the status has changed.

The help desk / back office should not change any existing ticket to this status.

No Time Entries can be logged against a ticket in this status.

- Status: Completed

This status indicates that one or more of the following conditions have been met including all Time Entries and notes up to date:

- The issue outlined in the ticket has been resolved or sufficiently alleviated.

- All work outlined or required has been completed.

- The client has not responded to requests about this ticket.

When a ticket is set to this status, the PSA system will send an email to the client contact indicated in the ticket, informing them that the status has changed.

No Time Entries can be logged against a ticket in this status.

- Status: Closed

This is used only by the Service Manager. Once it is verified that the ticket is completed and everything is correct in the ticket (notes, time entries, etc.), then the ticket is closed.

The process of closing tickets is often associated with invoicing or a similar once-a-week process. If you can do this cleanup every day, that would be great. But it's not required.

Note that "Closed" tickets will not show up in most reports. That's what you want! There's nothing worse than hundreds of tickets clogging up your reports when they should be closed and gone.

Implementation Notes

You might use this list of statuses as a starting place. But I highly recommend that you put together a list of statuses that reflect your business and your standard operating procedures. You should discuss these with your team and draw out a diagram that shows how tickets flow through your business, from "New" to "Closed."

As for the actual implementation, you need to be rigorous about flipping a switch and Just Do It.

Once you agree on your statuses, you need to jump in with both feet because it's the only way you can be absolutely sure that you know where all your tickets are at any given time. If you half-use the system, then you have no system. If the service manager excludes himself from the system, then you have no system. If the newbie techs don't have to follow the system, then you have no system.

The bottom line is, if you're going to define all these statuses, how they make your business work, etc., then you need to finish the job by implementing this standard operating procedure.

One of the great advantages of a PSA system is the ticket-tracking function. But you only get those advantages if you actually use it!

Three Take-Aways from This Chapter:

1. Create a list of statuses that reflects how you actually want your system to work.

2. If you find that you have unused statuses, determine whether you really need them at all. Have as few statuses as you need for smooth operation.

3. Give your technicians a "cheat sheet" so everyone knows exactly what these statuses mean.

Three Action Steps for Your Company:

1. _____

_____

2. _____

_____

3. _____

_____

7

Setting Job Priorities

The fundamental difference between "break/fix" computer support and managed services is planning your work. With break/fix, the standard operating system is to be constantly interrupted and to work on whatever the last thing is that fell in your lap.

Managed services allows you to schedule maintenance, and therefore avoid problems. And once problems arise, work should be prioritized. If you'd like two simple rules to make your business more successful and profitable, here they are:

1) All Work is done from service tickets

2) All tickets are worked from highest priority to lowest priority and from oldest to newest.

Overview

The basic flow of work within your office should be organized and standardized. As with everything else, you don't have to do it our way, but here are some thoughts.

Imagine that you have 1,000 service tickets in the system. You might be overwhelmed. Where do you start? Which do you work on first? The wrong answer is usually to work on the last thing that fell from the sky. That's called shoulder tap tech support and will keep you broke.

So, we prioritize all jobs from lowest to highest priority. Then we work on the highest priority tickets first. That assures that every technician is always working on the most important job. Once you do this, you'll be amazed at how much work you accomplish.

First you need some guidelines for setting priorities, and some basic examples that ring true in your business. Here are a few notes, As always, you need a human factor to fine-tune this. But this is a place to start.

There are four priority levels. We human beings only assign three of them (high, medium, and low).

Priority One Means Critical

A "P1" sets itself. That means …

- Server down

- Network down

- Email System down

- Server based Line of Business application down

- Fire, flood, earthquake, hazmat spill, etc.

Priority Two means High Priority

- Backups failing – 3 days in a row

- Company Communications (e.g., email is being blocked)

- Client has requested it be done within 24 hours or less

- Critical use workstation down
- The problem is inconveniencing everyone in the company
- The solution will significantly increase productivity for everyone in the company
- The issue is a result of other work recently done by us or another vendor
- The ticket has been open for more than 90 days

Priority Three means Medium Priority

- Backups failing – 2 days in a row
- One or more users productivity is significantly hindered
- The problem is inconveniencing multiple users
- Workstation down
- Client has requested it be done within 72 hours
- Secondary communications having problem (Blackberry, Droid, etc.)
- The ticket has been open for more than 60 days

Priority Four Means Low Priority

- Any item not having met the criteria for Priority 1,2 and 3 and not specifically requested by the client to be higher priority than to be done on the Weekly or Monthly Maintenance
- We often refer to this as "Scheduled" work with the clients

Notes:

The first thing you should notice is that we let clients set the priority (High/Medium/Low). With very few exceptions, clients don't abuse this. When necessary, we will adjust a priority. But, for the most part, we find that clients put things at a lower priority than we expected. We actually have clients say "Just do it the next time you're in."

The second thing you should notice is that "old" service requests are automatically elevated in priority. This is to prevent tickets from getting stale. You should use a PSA system and track the average age of tickets and the average time to close a ticket.

In reality, tickets just don't get too old. We haven't really had a problem with this. But it's a good practice to have in place, especially when you have a lot of new clients. The point of managed services is that clients will have fewer and fewer problems the longer they are on the system. So it's the new clients who have a high number of tickets.

Working Priorities

And what does it mean for a ticket to be P1, P2, P3, or P4?

P2 = High Priority

- Should be completed today before anything else. Must be completed before close of business, if possible.

P3 = Medium Priority

- Should be completed and closed within three business days. This is our default priority and this deadline is set automatically in the PSA when the ticket is created.

P4 = Low Priority

- Needs to be done, but there is no specific deadline. Usually these items are more of a reminder, such as Monthly Maintenance.

When tickets are assigned to a technician, or the tech is pulling tickets from a specific queue on your service board, the flow is the same:

- Find the highest priority tickets available to be worked (e.g., assigned to you, not on hold, and in a "workable" status. See the last chapter). Let's say this is a P1.

- If there is more than one ticket at this priority level, open the oldest ticket available to be worked.

- Work the ticket as far as you can go. That means anything from connecting remotely to working with vendor tech support. Whatever you can do, push this ticket as close to completion as you can.

- Go back to the queue and get another ticket:

- Find the highest priority ticket that is available to be worked. Find the oldest ticket at that level. Work that ticket.

- Rinse, repeat.

As you can see, this general flow means that you are always working on the highest priority ticket, and on the oldest tickets before the newer tickets.

This is one of the most important pieces of advice you will ever hear: **Everyone in your company should always be doing the highest priority thing they can be doing.**

Exceptions

There are a few common sense exceptions to this work flow.

First, if work is scheduled, then you need to stop working on other things and do the scheduled work. For example, if a vendor is going to be on the phone at 2:00 PM, or a client will be off her desktop machine at 11:00 AM. This obviously allows for a lot of that "low priority" work to be completed.

Second, if a technician is going onsite, he should list every open ticket at that client and attempt to work them all. Thus, if a client is going onsite for a P2 ticket, he might as well work every ticket he can. In some cases, a ticket is so low in priority that the client will say "No. We have to get out some newsletters. Do that another day." Okey dokey.

If you assign tickets:

In many shops, especially with lower volume, technicians just take the next available ticket. In some shops, the service coordinator or service manager assigns all work. We basically do 50/50. That allows us to be free-flowing when things are slow (or when the service manager is working on a P1 and everyone else is free-range). But we often have tickets assigned when it makes sense.

Here are a few notes if you assign tickets:

- Once assigned as the resource for a ticket, a tech is the owner of that ticket and ultimately responsible for its completion

- No work is performed on any ticket by a technician that is not assigned to that ticket without first checking with the tech who owns it

- Technicians first work all the tickets specifically assigned to them (from highest priority to lowest, and from oldest to newest)

  . . . then technicians grab tickets from the Service Board from highest priority to lowest and from oldest to newest

Implementation Notes

Whether you have a system or not, laying down the "rules" and procedures here is a pretty big task. It will require that you document your rules, as we've done with ours. Whether you use these or your own, you'll need to put together some handouts for your technicians. No one will remember all this.

This process makes sense once you work with it every day. But it will take some time and effort to actually implement and get it working the way it should. Hold a meeting. Describe the process. Use a white board for clarification. Address all the "what-if" and "but I" objections. Then implement. Just do it.

Benefits

This process takes some planning and commitment. It also takes dedication from the management team. If you don't believe in the system, you will never get technicians to believe in it.

When something goes wrong, evaluate it and figure out whether it was a one-time anomaly or whether you need to fine-tune your system. Ideally, with a system like this, Nothing gets old. Nothing gets lost. Nothing gets forgotten. And all the work gets done.

There are no specific forms for implementing this SOP, but the rules you decide on here must be programmed into your PSA system.

All of these systems allow for complicated and sophisticated work flows. Personally, I think you should keep it as simple as possible so that you don't create a small business bureaucracy . . . the worst kind there is!

Your PSA vendor should be able to help you implement your rules and procedures into their software.

Remember, the whole point of having processes and procedures is to make things run more smoothly. That will lead to more profit, more order, more efficiency, etc. BUT if the process is getting in the way of smooth operations, get the job done and then some back and fix the process.

Three Take-Aways from This Chapter:

1. Having every person in your company work from highest to lowest priority may be the most important SOP you ever adopt.

2. Priorities and expectations are related to one another. Define priorities and manage expectations.

3. Make sure that old tickets automatically become higher priority with age. This will keep you from ever having really old tickets!

Three Action Steps for Your Company:

1. _____

  _____

2. _____

  _____

3. _____

  _____

8

Service Ticket Updates

When you get a new service request (service ticket), there are several key pieces of information that will make your life easier. Some of these are the absolute basics of a service ticket (client, contract, priority, status).

Aside from a time entry itself, the service ticket needs to have some key information so that you can make your operation run more smoothly. Remember the old adage "garbage in/garbage out." You can't run any reports on data you don't collect! You can't take actions on data you don't put into the system. And, in this case, you will lose money if you don't have all the data you need.

Data you absolutely need to collect for each service ticket includes:

- Client Name / Contact Name

- Ticket / Job Title

- Desktop / User

- Priority of the Service Request (high, medium, low)

- Due Date

- Issue type (e.g., add/move/change or managed service)

- Issue Sub-Type (e.g., desktop, server, printer)

- Work Type (e.g., remote maintenance)

- Estimated Time to Complete Job

- Work Queue or service board

- Data that's nice to collect and may be useful includes:

    o   The Source of the service ticket (phone, email, tech talked to client, etc.)

    o   Is this a recurring issue?

If you have a PSA system such as Autotask, ConnectWise, or TigerPaw, then you are probably collecting most or all of this information. Certainly, you *could be* collecting it. If you have your own home-grown system, then you should try to make a point to collect this info.

But more importantly, every person who touches a service ticket should make sure this info is correct. Here's what I mean:

The most common ways that a service ticket enters our system are:

1) The client enters a service ticket through the client portal

2) The client sends us an email and it is parsed into a service ticket

3) A client calls on the phone and our office manager enters a service ticket

4) A client talks to a tech and the tech enters a service ticket

In each case, it is likely that the office manager and a technician will open and look at a service ticket before the service manager. The service manager will eventually open the service ticket if it hasn't already been worked and closed by the time he goes to sort through the service board.

Implementation Notes

Each person who touches the service ticket is responsible for entering information into the "required" fields above. The two items most likely to be skipped are marked with an asterisk – setting the priority and setting the time estimate. Oddly enough, these are two of the most important fields.

We work all jobs based on their priority. Therefore, each service ticket must have a priority! You cannot work jobs in the right order if the most important variable for sorting is missing! The time estimate is critical to estimating your backlog and for scheduling. We ask our office manager to simply enter one hour into this field if it is blank or she has no information to go on. That is normally a high estimate, but it's better than a zero!

Because the service manager massages the service board at least once a day (see Chapter Eleven), he will always check the time estimate on every service ticket he touches. So the time estimate will become accurate in short order.

Benefits

Eventually you will want to run reports to tell you whether a specific client is profitable, whether a specific piece of client equipment is troublesome, the average close time for a service ticket, the number of "Priority One" tickets in the system, and so forth. With a PSA system you have an amazing amount of information about your own business. But you have to put the information in if you plan to get it out.

One of the key pieces of information is your backlog: How many hours of labor do you have in the system? Backlog is determined by the total hours remaining on all the service tickets. You also need to track the billability of your technicians. The calculation looks like this:

Backlog = hours to be worked x billability of techs

Let's say your average tech is 60% billable (in a 40 hour week, they put in 24 hours of billable labor). And let's say you have 240 hours of estimated labor in your service board. Therefore, you need to plan having 400 hours of labor available in order to finish that work.

These calculations will tell you whether your backlog is likely to shrink or grow over time, based on the labor you have available. These can help you decide whether to cut hours or hire a new tech.

If you have a PSA, the "forms" you need to implement this SOP are built in. Otherwise, you'll need to create a tracking system of some kind that includes the key variables above.

Implementing this policy is pretty simple. Just have everyone who touches a service ticket go through the key fields and adjust as needed. You might even take a screen shot of the "New Ticket" screen and highlight the fields that you require. Give each tech, and the office manager, a copy.

Three Take-Aways from This Chapter:

1. Begin entering this key information into every ticket, every time it is touched.

2. Once you have just one month of good record keeping, you will be able to generate some meaningful reports about your company and your technicians.

3. Everyone on your team needs to reinforce this policy. Ask "Is the ticket up to date" – all the time – all day long.

Three Action Steps for Your Company:

1. _____

_____

2. _____

_____

3. _____

_____

9

Time Entry and Note Entry in Service Tickets

The notes and time entries in your ticketing system are perhaps the most important documentation that exists within your service department. It's the key to solving problems, defending your billing, justifying payroll, and much more. As a result, you need some standard procedures about entering service notes (time entries).

In a sense, your ticketing system/CRM is a massive asynchronous communications system. If you work in real time (see Volume Three, Chapter Four), the service board will always reflect the exact state of your service delivery. You'll be able to watch tickets open, close, and all the statuses in between.

Here are the key things a technician needs to do with each time entry (case note):

1) Triage the ticket as described in the last chapter. This means that the first thing the tech needs to do is to verify that they key fields of the ticket are still accurate. Is it the right description, in the right queue, with the correct status, etc.?

2) Client notes should be in every time entry/case note. These are notes that would be visible to the client either on an invoice or in a report. The client may never read these. Sometimes I think no client ever reads these. Then I get a client complaining because

she didn't get a report last month. So she expects one, even if she doesn't read it.

The point is: A client might see these notes.

Whether or not the client sees the notes, the service manager will. So they should be good. Talk about what you did and focus on the fix, not the road that got there. The notes should be as minimal as possible, but enough to justify the billing.

3) Internal notes are not required. But sometimes it's useful to have direct communications between the tech in the field and the service manager. Appropriate notes might be: "This printer grabs a new IP address all the time. We should either hard code it or figure out what's going on with DHCP." Inappropriate: "Client is stupid. We've shown her how to do this four or five times."

Treat internal notes like Facebook. Assume it's private right now. But also assume that one day everything you type here will be indexed and widely available. So keep it professional and constructive.

4) Time Entries should be accurate. You company should have a policy about the time increments you use (e.g., 15 minutes) and time entries should be consistent with that. See Volume Three, Chapter Seventeen: *Time Tracking for Employees.*

5) WITNS. There's a key item we like to see on every tick that is not closed: "What is the next step?" – WITNS. There are lots of

reasons why tickets do not close. It is five o'clock and you'll be back in the morning; you're waiting on parts; you've passed the issue to Sales; you're waiting on a vendor; you've done what you can do and you need to escalate; etc.

When a ticket does not close for whatever reason, the tech should give some guidance to the next person who will open that ticket. Do we need to schedule a memory test? Does the sales manager need to talk to the client? Are we waiting on parts?

A great example involves going through a New PC checklist. If a tech finished half the job and goes to lunch, where can I pick up that job and finish with as little re-work as possible? WITNS tells me that information.

6) Documented Work. Every time entry – whether the case is closed or not – should end with the phrase "Documented Work." This means three things within your company: First, it means the tech put these notes into the system before leaving the client's office. Second, it means the technician is working in real time. Third, it means that all relevant information has been entered into the appropriate documentation. This might be paper documentation onsite, documentation online (such as a SharePoint site), in the CRM, or simply in the case notes.

I have no idea what it means to the client. But it sounds good.

If you've never taken time entries (case notes) seriously before, you should. They are a critical element of communication. They require a certain level of precision. And they are a good way to make sure that the service manager is tuned in to what's going on at the client's office.

Imagine the telephone conversation when the service manager has no knowledge of a service request, but he can bring up the case notes and understand exactly what went on. That allows him to have a productive conversation with the client and sound like he DOES know what's going on with the network.

As always, you don't need to do things exactly this way. But you should do them very consistently and systematically within your service department.

Three Take-Aways from This Chapter:

1. Your ticketing system is an excellent tool for asynchronous communications within your company.

2. Every ticket you do not close should have a WITNS entry: What is the next step?

3. Every time entry should conclude with the phrase "Documented Work."

Three Action Steps for Your Company:

1. _____

_____

2. _____

_____

3. _____

_____

10

Information Sharing

Information is the backbone of our industry. In fact, "IS" or Information Systems used to be what this industry was called. Now it's called "IT" – Information Technology. So what are we about? What do we do? We design, build, and support the infrastructure that makes information usable.

It seems fitting that we should manage our internal information as effectively as we manage our clients' information systems. And like everything else, we need to document our processes.

There are many ways that teams share information. You might use SharePoint, shared drive space, or keep notes inside your CRM. Ideally, you will use some combination of all of these. In addition, you will have printouts. I know, everyone says they want the paperless office. And we use a lot less paper than ever before. But the truly paperless office will arrive shortly after the paperless bathroom.

You need policies about how your team will share information for the same reason that you need an SOP for where you will store data. Remember the policy about the !Tech Directory (See Volume Two, Chapter Twenty-Nine)? That policy allows everyone on the team to know exactly where to look for certain information (in this cases software and drivers).

If you don't have a standardized policy then, by definition, everyone on the team will put stuff wherever it makes sense to them at the moment they are saving data. So one person will store documents in their personal folders, a second person put throw up spreadsheets on the SharePoint site, and a third will use the common department share on the cloud drive.

And when you go looking for that information, where will you look? You certainly won't look in someone else's personal folders. Will you look on the server share? In SharePoint? Or within the CRM/PSA? Unless you're a mind reader, you will waste time looking for information – every single time you need it.

Document Types and Sub-Types

Personally, I think the easiest way to organize data is to start with the team or function. Then, within that, you can sort by project or file type. For example, your shared public folders on the server might include individual sub-folders for marketing, finance, tech support, etc. See the chapter on *Organizing Company Files and Folders* (Volume Two, Chapter Twenty-Eight).

Within each team folder, you can then divide documents in a way that makes the most sense. For some documents that means by project, for others it is by month. Additional sub-folders might be for clients, legal, drafts, etc. The key thing is to choose ONE organization method per team and stick with it. It should make sense to everyone on that team.

You will know you're successful if documents are consistently in the first place you look for them.

Team Standards

Once you divide information by teams, you need to set up standards for each team. This is necessary because teams will access information in different ways. For example, our tech support team stores most client-related checklists on a SharePoint drive so we have total access to them while we're in the field. Because we don't map client computers to our cloud storage, getting files from the cloud drive is a little more cumbersome.

All of our other teams work out of the office. Finance, office management, and sales are all connected to mapped drives all the time, so they have no real need for SharePoint.

Specific information is stored in the CRM/PSA. This consists primarily of information about client configurations (routers, firewalls, etc.). The PSA is hosted and therefore available from everywhere. So technicians can easily access this information in the field. Similarly, certain information from the Sales Team is also put into the PSA for easy access by the technicians. For example, license documents and keys will be added to a client's configuration information by the sales person as soon as we get it. That way the technician will have it when he goes to install software.

Team Policies

Don't get carried away thinking this has to be a big, formal policy. One sentence for each type of information is all you need.

I recommend that you create a document for each distinct team that simply lists the kinds of information you normally deal with and where it is stored. This is basically a "cheat sheet" that new employees can use until they instinctively know where to put things. It's also useful for documents that are rarely used, such as quarterly or annual reports.

As your mother (or somebody) used to say: "A place for everything and everything in its place."

Three Take-Aways from This Chapter:

1. Each team should have a very short statement of policy about where they store the documents they use most frequently.

2. Create a little cheat-sheet for new employees. It's not bad for long-timers as well.

3. When you go to look for a document, it should be in the first place you look. If it's not, consider whether you need to update this policy.

Three Action Steps for Your Company:

1. _____

   _____

2. _____

   _____

3. _____

   _____

11

Massaging the Service Board

In the field of statistical research, there's a term called "massaging the numbers" or massaging the data. You see, after you've collected the data, they just exist. And despite what news pundits and politicians want you to believe, the data do not speak for themselves. You have to coax the meaning out of them.

Your service board is the same way.

The service tickets and internal tasks in your service board need to be managed like a living entity. Tickets move from status to status, and from queue to queue. If you're not careful, things can get lost. One of the main reasons you have a ticketing system is so that things don't get lost. But that's not magic.

And so we have the term "Massaging the Service Board."

Note: This chapter synthesizes a good deal of what we've been working up to in this four-book set. Please forgive the references to earlier chapters. I tried to keep these to a minimum. But you'll see that this is where all those PSA posts begin to come together. You'll also see that it takes some practice to keep all those procedures in your head at once.

To be honest, that's why we have a service manager or a service coordinator. Someone has to remember all this (or have a checklist).

But you don't need every technician to be able to do all this. Let them do what they do best.

Overview

First, how can things get "lost" in your service board? Well, there are several kinds of lost:

An item can sit in a waiting status (see Chapter Six) and never be seen again. This is particularly true of *Waiting on Client*.

A ticket can be mis-handled by technicians. The most common example of this is when one tech opens a ticket, pokes around, and determines that he can't move it forward (or he's just too lazy to take on the task). He logs 15 minutes for doing nothing. Then another tech does the same thing. And another. And another. Then the first guy again. Soon you've got two hours of labor that's not real labor . . . and the ticket hasn't moved.

If the service manager or coordinator aren't familiar with the board, they may not know where to look for all the tickets. This is more of a danger if you have too many queues, too many statuses, too many work types, etc.

Sometimes old tickets or even low priority tickets don't get the attention they deserve. Some clients fear that their low priority tickets will never be addressed, so you need to make sure you take care of these.

Some tickets are hidden by the system unless you are the assigned technician. Unless you have a very large shop, I don't recommend this. At any rate the service manager or coordinator needs to see everything.

The Basic Massage

Just like a good back rub, the basic massage will make your service board feel better right away. The basic massage consists of looking at all of the new tickets very quickly. Basically, you're going to do a quick check to verify that all the fields are right. See Chapter Eight on *Service Ticket Updates*.

Next, you'll sort all open tickets from oldest to newest. How old is the oldest ticket? If it's one week, someone's deleting tickets and you need to find out who it is so you can fire them.

Seriously, though. How many tickets are more than 30 days old? 60? 90? If you follow the advice I gave in Chapter Seven, then you'll move these older tickets up in priority.

It is VERY important to track the average age of tickets.

- The average age of all tickets at time of closing

- The average age of all tickets with Priority One

- The average age of all tickets with Priority Two

- The average age of all tickets with Priority Three

- The average age of all tickets with Priority Four

PSA systems promise that you'll be able to do all kinds of reporting. But, as a rule, their reporting is clunky and difficult for things like this. If you generate reports for things like the age of a ticket, you're pretty safe. But it's always a good idea to go dig up the data and verify the math yourself for a few reports to make sure you're actually measuring what you want and that the system is giving you correct data.

. . . So back to the basic massage . . .

Your focus right now should be on the oldest tickets. Make sure that they are getting attention and that they don't languish. You might from time to time give a senior technician a couple of really old tickets and make sure they're handled ASAP.

Next, you'll sort the tickets by priority. How many Priority Ones are in the system? P2? P3? P4? Log this information so you can track it over time. You might want to enter these counts into an Excel spreadsheet on Friday at 5PM, or some other regular day and time.

Note that you will eventually get a real "feel" for your ticketing system when you notice that new tickets are being prioritized correctly when they're created. You'll know this because you'll have more P4s than P3s, more P3s than P2s, and almost no P1s. That should be your norm.

Make sure the highest priority tickets are getting the most attention. That means schedule them, find out where they are, and re-arrange technicians to keep the focus on the highest priority tickets.

Remember, we work tickets *from highest priority to lowest priority*, from *oldest to newest*.

Finally, you want to look at all the tickets that had time entries OR were closed yesterday (the previous work day). Did the technician communicate with the client? Does the time look right? Does the client need a little note saying "Hey, hope everything's working great with that printer"? And so forth.

Massage the clients while you're massaging the board.

Deep Issue Massage

Just like a deep tissue massage, your board sometimes needs a Deep Issue Massage. You'll do the basic massage every day. It shouldn't take long. 30-60 minutes max . . . if you do it every day. The Deep Issue Massage takes a little longer. You might want to do it every week or so.

First, look at each queue or service board. Look at each ticket assigned to your Back Office (such as Continuum, Dove Help Desk, Third Tier, etc. – see www.continuum.net, www.dovehelpdesk.com, and www.thirdtier.net). Are these tickets being addressed appropriately? Are they moving forward? Close anything that's completed but just sitting around for a long time waiting for someone to approve closing it.

Second, look at the billable tickets. These should all be scheduled, or at least have notes about when they can be scheduled. No matter what the priority, truly billable labor (as opposed to managed service labor) needs to be scheduled on a regular basis.

Third, check out the internal admin tickets. This is where your employees log their time for straightening out their desk, checking email, sitting on webinars, and other activities you can't bill to a client. Yes, you need this. But these activities really need to be kept in check.

Our experience is that a handful of technicians will have really high "admin" time and others will have near zero. Guess which ones are better techs? But you need to check in on this in order to keep yourself informed. Make notes and have talks as needed.

Fourth, check your "escalated" tickets. That means the ones thrown to the most senior techs because 1) No one else can do it, 2) The problem is old or very difficult, or 3) a critical issue has been going on for some time and you're working with a third party support desk.

Escalated tickets can kill your profitability. If they drag on, you need to figure out what else you can do to fix the problem and move on. Don't harp on the tech every day, but do bring it up once a week.

This is also a great time to see if you've totally over-worked one tech with a bunch of crises. Manage the people part of your business as well.

Fifth, review special projects. This includes migrations, new installs, client on-boarding, and whatever else you've got going. Is all time being properly logged to these projects? If you follow the process outlined in the book *Project Management in Small Business* (by Dana Goulston, PMP, and me), then you need to make sure that all time is logged to the appropriate tickets/tasks within the project.

Obviously, you want to make sure that the project is moving forward and looking successful. Again, a little client contact might be in order. Don't bug them every day, but make sure the actions and attitudes are all aligned for success at least once a week.

Make changes as needed to assign or re-assign technicians to keep all projects moving forward. Close tickets and project "stages" as appropriate. Massage the project.

Sixth, review scheduled maintenance. That's your monthly maintenance, weekly maintenance, quarterly maintenance, etc. Anything that's scheduled and recurring.

Here, you want to make sure that things are being scheduled and executed in a timely fashion. If it's the 25th of the month, you better not be 1/3 of the way finished with monthly maintenance tickets! If you've skipped monthly maintenance at a client or two, that's a real danger sign.

For some reason (at least in our company) there always seem to be monthly maintenance tickets that remain open even when the work is done. Perhaps techs think the service coordinator should close them. Perhaps the tech was waiting on a report or a successful restore. For whatever reason, it appears that everything is complete, but the ticket's still open. Ping the tech and close the ticket. This will clean up your stats, too.

Seventh, look through the sales tickets (pre-sales, post sales, or whatever). Are your sales people getting the support they need from technicians? Are quotes going out to clients and prospects in a timely manner?

Note: We talked about "sales tickets" and sales queues in Volume One, Chapter Thirty-Nine. Here are samples of what we mean.

Example pre-sales ticket: Technician is onsite and client says they want a quote for a new printer. The tech enters a ticket with a note that it should be assigned to sales. In our system, new tickets always go through the client access queue. From there, the person monitoring the board acknowledges the ticket, puts it in the right queue, assigns it, etc. (Recall the discussion of *Service Ticket Updates* in Chapter Eight).

Example post-sales ticket: After the client gets a quote and approves the quote, the ticket is moved to post-sales. The sales person still has to receive payment, then order the equipment. The ticket has statuses of waiting on client, waiting on vendor, or something similar. Once the equipment arrives, the ticket is moved to the status "Schedule This" and moved to the appropriate work queue or service board.

Implementation Notes

Final notes on the Deep Issue Massage:

This can be a half-day project when you first do it. It will go faster over time. In a perfect world, you will get in the groove of massaging the service board a little every day and that will make the big massage a lot faster.

Basically, you want to have someone be able to have a sense of how all the tickets in your company are flowing. It IS a lot of work at first, but becomes much easier if you do it every day.

The weekly Deep Issue Massage is also a great time to generate the statistics you need to calculate your backlog. If all the numbers are right in all the tickets, you should be able to calculate the total number of hours you need to close all the tickets, and the rate at which you are closing tickets. Of course new tickets will always enter the system, but the goal is to come up with a backlog number that's reasonable, sustainable, and profitable for you.

In the next chapter we'll talk about managing the backlog, but for now, just start keeping those stats.

Benefits

The primary benefit of massaging your service board is that you keep it under control. You verify that your company is using the PSA system. You verify that you are meeting your promises to clients. You verify that you don't have a bunch of old tickets out there.

You guarantee that things are flowing . . . and profitable.

In the normal course of massaging the service board, you will close a number of tickets that should have been closed. You'll straighten out priorities. You'll schedule your technicians better. And you'll do some good client relationship management.

There are no specific forms for implementing this SOP. You might write up a brief description of the procedure and put it into your SOP or binder.

This kind of policy requires that everyone on the team be aware of the policy and support it.

It requires one or two people to have the skills to massage the board.

Three Take-Aways from This Chapter:

1. Even if you look at the service board every day, tickets can hide. Massaging the service board will help you to see them.

2. After just two weeks of massaging the service board, any "out of control" system should be neat and tidy.

3. Once you have actual numbers to work with, you will be able to anticipate the flow of tickets – and labor – into, through, and out of your service department. This is powerful information.

Three Action Steps for Your Company:

1. _____

    _____

2. _____

    _____

3. _____

    _____

12

Service Board Backlog Management

With luck, you are very busy with lots of service requests. If not, I hope you will be soon!

When you have a busy service board, it is important to make sure that you don't lose something "between the cracks." Here's a process to take care of that and then attack any backlog that may exist. Please note: A backlog is not bad! It's better to know that all your techs are busy than to have pockets of inactivity.

This process is to be completed by the Tech Support Manager/Service Manager or the Service Coordinator. It should be somebody that can make decisions to re-allocate resources to get tickets un-stuck and moving toward completion.

The Service Board needs constant attention, but the complete process of prioritizing, assigning and scheduling resources really needs to be done at most two or three times a week. Early Monday AM is a must and toward the end of the week is good to help bring the next week into focus. See the last chapter.

Since all SR's are to be acknowledged within a set time of creation during business hours, that process is at the top of the to-do list.

Note: When new service requests enter the system (created by clients or your technicians), you need to always go through the process described in Chapter Eight, *Service Ticket Updates.*

Basically, the goal is that that service coordinator – and everyone who touches the ticket – needs to verify the ticket title, priority, work type, service agreement, etc. Here's the result of that process: Every time you touch an SR, you update as many fields as possible. So, the next time you refine your search in an attempt to reveal SRs needing attention, you actually find fewer tickets that need attention.

What you'll see in a minute is that we use a variety of sorting methods to view all the tickets. The reason for reviewing the entire list of SRs after changing the sort order is to be sure that you have a complete understanding of the overall workload on your company and the needs of the clients. If the list is viewed in several different ways this will become apparent.

While reviewing SRs, request a Status update from the assigned tech(s) on any SR that is believed to either be in the wrong status, incomplete, or has incorrect information.

Don't Be Overwhelmed

If you don't regularly massage your service board or review tickets, you might have a huge number of tickets that need to be cleaned up. If you have totally neglected your service board, it might take you a whole business day to go through this the first time. But four days later, it will be much cleaner and easier.

The following Monday, this process will actually be pretty fast. This is due in large part to the fact that you've now touched every ticket in the system at least once in the previous seven days and you know which tickets are correct and don't need to be evaluated again.

The first time you go through this, be sure to read each step very carefully and do exactly what it says. After you've gone through the process 3-4 times, you'll get by with just a checklist that says

- Acknowledge New Tickets
- Review Completed Tickets
- Sort by Priority
- Sort by Age
- Sort by Hours
- Sort by Status
- Schedule Work

Eventually, this will become second nature, you will have a very good handle on your board, and it will take less than half an hour.

Note also that the first time you go through this process, you will move many tickets to "Closed" or "Completed" status. You'll re-prioritize a lot of tickets. You will probably combine some tickets into one. And you'll set reasonable time budgets for all tickets.

That will be a huge relief and greatly diminish your perceived backlog. Through this process, you'll learn about your PSA system, how tickets flow through your system, and what you need your technicians to do better.

Of course you will fine-tune this process based on your ticket statuses and procedures. This is a place to start.

Tackling the Ticket Backlog

Step One: Open the Service Board and review the Primary Sort.

Our Service Board is set up with a default sort of "By Status." With this, you can determine which status you want first, second, third, etc. We have the system put "New" status on the top, followed by:

- Acknowledged

- Assigned

- Schedule This

- Scheduled

- In Progress

- Waiting . . . (Results, materials, customer, vendor)

- Customer Reply

- On Hold

- Completed

Step Two: Acknowledge each New Service Request as detailed in the Acknowledging New SRs procedure.

Step Three: Review all SRs in the Completed Status.

Tune up these SRs as follows:

- Verify that everything is in order and update as necessary

- Review the time entries and other pertinent information

- Pay close attention to all time entries and the Service Agreement applied to the ticket. These determine whether the work will be billed or not.

- Change the status to Completed when all fields and notes have been updated

Step Four: Sort the Board by Priority (Highest to Lowest) and review the entire list of SRs.

- Review the entire list to verify correct priority

- Pay close attention to the age of high priority SRs and why they are getting older

- Update other fields as necessary

Step Five: Sort the Board by Age and review the entire list of SRs.

- On Mondays (or the first day of the week) pay close attention to SRs that are 0 to 3 days old as they have come in over the weekend and need to be addressed right away

- Verify that any SR over 60 days old is at Priority 3. Update other fields as necessary.

- Verify that any SR over 90 days old is at Priority 2. Update other fields as necessary.

Step Six: Sort the Board by Budget Hours and review all SRs with a Budget of 0 hours remaining.

- Estimate and update the Budgeted Hours

- Update other fields as necessary

- Starting from the bottom of the list (largest budget hours) review all SRs that are over budget.

- Update other fields as necessary

Step Seven: Sort the Board by Status again and review all SRs in the following order. Scrutinize the status and update as necessary.

- In Progress – Verify the status is still valid and update as needed. Is it moving forward right now?

- Scheduled – Only items with a status of Scheduled that have a scheduled date in the past need to be reviewed. It is most important that if the schedule was missed or moved that it be re-scheduled immediately. If necessary, determine why the SR was not worked when scheduled.

- Acknowledged – These tickets need to be moved to Assigned, Scheduled, or some other status that will move them forward.

- On Hold – Only the Service Manager can place a ticket on hold. This basically means that no one should work on the ticket until further notice. If there are tickets on hold, determine whether this is still appropriate. For example, if you are waiting for a payment from the client, you might leave a ticket on hold.

Step Eight: Assign tickets to technicians and schedule work that needs to be done on a specific day or at a specific time.

- If status is Schedule This: Work from highest priority to lowest and from oldest to newest. It is the best practice to schedule the technician who is already assigned to the SR if the work is an ongoing issue that would not easily be passed from one technician to another.

- Sort the Board by Required Date. Verify that all tickets with a due date approaching are assigned to a technician so we don't miss the required target.

In general, you should be following the flow of tickets through your system that we defined earlier in Chapters Four, Six, Seven, and

Eight. The process of managing backlog and massaging the service board is intended to make sure that all tickets are moving appropriately through the system. You should never be happy with "stuck" tickets.

It may help to picture the paths through your service board like a giant board game. There are several paths that can be taken. There are detours and shortcuts. Sometimes you have to go backward, but the general flow is always forward. Eventually, every ticket moves through the system and off the board.

And everybody wins. ☺

Notes

There are no specific forms for implementing this SOP. You should write up a brief checklist, based on what we've presented here. Everyone who might be called upon to go through this process should do it at least once with a supervisor before being left to do it on their own.

It is important that you keep track of the total number of backlog hours. It will almost always be shorter when you are finished with this process.

Sometimes you will increase the backlog because you have tickets with zero estimated time remaining and you need to add hours to that. But, more often, you will find some tickets that are almost done, or completely finished. So you will reduce the hours on these or close them altogether.

Whether the backlog increases or decreases, you should track it and chart it at least once per week. Put that chart on the wall in the service department.

:

Three Take-Aways from This Chapter:

1. Backlog of work is one of the key health indicators in your business. Track it rigorously.

2. The point of keeping backlog under control is to provide excellent service and verify that you know the current state of your service board.

3. Once the backlog is under control, you'll know what is normal. You can't return to normal until you know what it is. And if normal changes, you'll only be aware of that because you are aware of what it used to be.

Three Action Steps for Your Company:

1. _____

    _____

2. _____

    _____

3. _____

    _____

13

Daily Monitoring of Client Machines

What is the "guts" of managed services? It's managing client systems. Monitoring, automated ticketing, patching, fixing, and applying updates. It's preventive maintenance. In my book *Service Agreements for SMB Consultants: A Quick-Start Guide to Managed Services,* I talk about building a "roll your own" monitoring system with Small Business Server and a few other tools. That system works very well. But whether you use a system like that or invest in GFI Max, Continuum, LabTech, or something else, the daily monitoring is critical to delivering on the promises of managed service.

As with any other tools, you can set up all the alerts and monitoring you want. With the right combination you can even have tickets created automatically. But if you don't actively manage that whole system, then you're not really doing what you need to do.

Okay, so what does it mean to *actively manage*? Basically, it means that you check to make sure things are working. When they're not, you create service tickets. When problems keep recurring, you escalate the issue. Here's a simple checklist. I'm going to assume you have a remote monitoring and management tool (RMM). If you do not, then you will have to manually check each of these items.

Note on the Exchange "Monitor" folder: If you have reports emailed to you from an old Small Business Server or various backup programs, set the email to a mail-enabled public folder named

Monitor. That way, you will have all such reports in one place and you can easily address them and then move the emails to the appropriate client folder.

I won't go into a lecture about how important backups are. You already know that.

[Insert your personal rant about backups here.]

Checklist: Daily Backup Monitoring of Client Systems

1. Check the "all in one" report on system backups

    a. Open the Daily Backup Monitoring Record spreadsheet located on SharePoint at "Tech Documents\Daily Monitoring Record.xlsx" and update the previous night's column with backup successes and failures. (A sample of this Excel document is included in the downloadable material that accompanies this book.)

2. Sort the Monitor mailbox in Exchange Public Folders and make necessary edits to the Daily Monitoring Record spreadsheet

    a. Be sure to check to see if there were any old backup jobs marked with an 'R' and replace it with an 'X' or 'O' if they completed or failed.

    b. Once documented, move all emails to their respective client folders so the Monitor folder is empty.

    c. If there are backups that were not accounted for in both Monitor email box and the RMM portal, login to the server itself and check the backup software for the status of the backups. Update the Daily Monitoring Record with findings.

    d. Create Service Requests (tickets) as needed and set them to the appropriate priority (see below).

    e. If you have an outsourced help desk, add all necessary criteria to SRs so that the help desk shouldn't have to ask for further information. Then assign all such tickets to the help desk to investigate.

3. Review all Backup related tickets in the PSA and move them forward

    a. Check SRs to see if help desk is waiting for information or action by us.

    b. If a backup job has failed more than once, adjust the priority as needed.

    c. If a backup fails four days in a row and has been assigned to the outsourced help desk, take it back in-house and send an urgent email to the service manager.

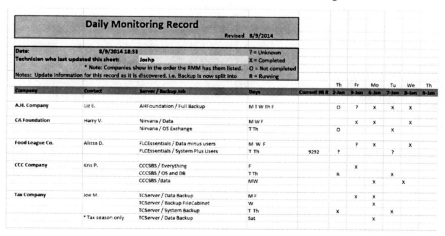

Daily Monitoring Record — Revised 8/9/2014

Date: 8/9/2014 18:53				? = Unknown
Technician who last updated this sheet: Joshp				X = Completed
* Note: Companies show in the order the RMM has them listed.				O = Not completed
Notes: Update information for this record as it is discovered. i.e. Backup is now split into				R = Running

					Th	Fr	Mo	Tu	We	Th
Company	Contact	Server / Backup Job	Days	Current 98 #	2-Jan	3-Jan	6-Jan	7-Jan	8-Jan	9-Jan
A.H. Company	Liz E.	AHFoundation / Full Backup	M T W Th F		O	?	X	X	X	
CA Foundation	Harry V.	Nirvana / Data	M W F			X	X		X	
		Nirvana / OS Exchange	T Th		O			X		
Food League Co.	Alissa D.	FLCEssentials / Data minus users	M W F			?	X		X	
		FLCEssentials / System Plus Users	T Th	9292	?			?		
CCC Company	Kris P.	CCCSBS / Everything	F			X				
		CCCSBS / OS and DB	T Th		R			X		
		CCCSBS /data	MW				X	X		
Tax Company	Joe M.	TCServer / Data Backup	M F			X	X			
		TCServer / Backup FileCabinet	W				X			
		TCServer / System Backup	T Th		X			X		
	* Tax season only	TCServer / Data Backup	Sat				X			

Backup Jobs and Ticket Priorities

Note the SOP on setting ticket priorities: If a backup fails once, the ticket is created as Priority 3 (medium). If it fails twice in a row, you can leave it at P3 as we do, or you might decide to move to P2. If a backup fails three days in a row, it must be a P2 (high priority). See the discussion of setting priorities for service tickets in Chapter Seven.

You should have lots of backups (at least one per client), so do not let failed backup jobs go unattended! There are very few things that jump right to the top of your priority list: a failed backup is one!

Daily attention matters! When you track backups every day, you quickly learn the little quirks in each client system. This is particularly true when a specific piece of software mis-reports the results of a backup job. Grrrr. Annoying, but at least you know your system works even if the software is having problems.

It is extremely rare for a client to respect the importance of backups. Even though it's in their best interest, they just don't comprehend how critical backups are. Of course it's not their job to care: That's what they're paying you for.

Other Daily Monitoring

With your RMM tool, you should be monitoring all key functions on client machines. These are an automated, minute-by-minute version of the things you should be checking on in your monthly maintenance checklist (disc space, processor usage, stopped services, critical events, etc.). For a sample of things to monitor, see the downloadable version of the 68-Point Checklist discussed in Volume Three, Chapter Three.

For the most part, daily monitoring of desktop machines is very basic. Other than virus updates and Windows updates, there's not much that needs to be monitored. You should be able to find (or create) a dashboard in your RMM so you can view all desktops/laptops with green, yellow, and red dots.

Servers should also be basic, but of course they're more important. Each server has at least one critical function, so you need to verify that that function is working, along with the basics of disc usage, services, etc. Again, a nice dashboard with lights goes a long way. See the graph.

Just as with backups, your daily once-over of the servers will keep you in touch with the weird stuff that somehow develops in some machines. You'd think that every Server 2012 Standard with the same hardware, same patch level, and same hard drives would be the same . . . but Noooooooooooo . . .

Time and Tickets

It is important that service tickets are created for any work to be performed. The task of daily monitoring is an administrative task and the time should be logged to an internal ticket. For each client task that needs to be performed, a separate client ticket should be created. If your systems are patched up as they should be, the daily monitoring should take no more than 15-30 minutes for 1,000 machines monitored. Do not let the tech get side-tracked into fixing things at this point and muddling up the time.

Remember the mantra: **All work is performed against a service ticket!** That means the tech who does daily monitoring can create tickets, but must not work them at this time. Once daily monitoring is complete, any new tickets will be in the system, prioritized properly. Who knows? By the time the monitoring task is finished, the service manager may have already assigned some new tickets, or even worked them.

Anyway, daily monitoring is critical to keeping your fingers on the pulse of your clients' machines. It also allows you to create service tickets, work them, and close them before the client is aware that there was an issue. Just make sure they get a report each month telling them all the wonderful things you do without their knowledge.

Three Take-Aways from This Chapter:

1. Monitoring is not the time to fix things. If things need to be fixed, create a service request.

2. An argument can be made that monitoring backups is the most important function you perform. It should be done for every client, every day.

3. The ultimate goal of managed services is to make every run more smoothly. One critical piece of this is daily monitoring with quick response.

Three Action Steps for Your Company:

1. _____

_____

2. _____

_____

3. _____

_____

14

Patch Management Philosophy and Procedures

Whether you practice break/fix or managed services, it is a best practice to keep client computers as well maintained as possible. And while I prefer automated, perpetual maintenance, that's not practical for everyone. Let's look at three aspects of patch management:

1) Philosophy

2) Manual

3) Automated

Patch Management Philosophy

I know some people think "philosophy" seems out of place in the world of technology. But we all have some philosophies that guide us. For example, when do you sell a new operating system? It used to be common wisdom that you don't install a new version of Windows until Service Pack 1 is released. That hasn't been true for a long time. For more than ten years now, Microsoft has had massive public beta programs that put their O.S. in the hands of millions of users for many months before the release date. So the release version is very stable.

Service packs are another story. Here, too, Microsoft has improved dramatically. But there's still good reason to wait. First, SPs are 98%

just a collection of previously released fixes. So a well-patched machine will have the critical elements. As a result, modern SPs provide a certain level of consistency and stability, but their deployment is not critical.

For non-Microsoft service packs and patches, we're more leery. Because we don't see them as often or as consistently, we don't know how reliable or safe they are. As a result, we are very careful with installs and very watchful when we perform them.

If you support a specific application, you may know it's quirks and patterns. If so, you may have a philosophy for that application. If not, then fall back to the more generic (careful) philosophy for lesser-known application updates.

One final example has emerged in recent years: The Zero Day Attack. These are viruses or attacks that become widely known on the same day. There is no time (zero days) to prepare for the attack. Sounds like there's nothing you can do? Not true. As long as you talk about WHAT you will do when the day comes, you can have some level of preparedness.

In this case the SOP involves having pre-defined lines of command and communication. When a zero day attack happens, who will decide how your company responds? How will you communicate with the team? How will you communicate with the clients?

As I said, we all have these philosophies. And every technician you hire has a set of philosophies as well. But each company needs to operate on one philosophy. If you're the owner, or service manager, then YOUR philosophy is the one that matters. You need to write it out and educate the rest of the team.

When major service packs or patches come out, you need to orchestrate a plan for installing them. This probably means creating one service request for each client server or one SR for each client.

You might schedule these for the same time as the monthly maintenance, or maybe assign the whole lot to one or two technicians.

The key to success is that you 1) Have a philosophy, and 2) Propagate it to your staff. This is best accomplished by writing out your philosophies and putting them in your SOP document/folder. After that, you need to have a training, talk this out with your staff, and agree on how you'll proceed.

Manual Patch Management

If you do not have an RMM (remote monitoring and management) system such as GFI Max, Continuum, or LabTech, then you will be installing these updates "by hand." Alternatively, one of your philosophies may be to enable automatic updates from Microsoft. But you still need to apply updates to Office applications. Many non-critical updates won't be applied by automatic updates. And, of course, you need to apply updates to all those non-Microsoft products as well.

If you don't have an RMM system, you will have to create a schedule for updates.

One possible policy is to apply updates whenever you find yourself logged into a client computer. That's not bad, but if you do this, make sure you keep a list of all updates for that client on the c:\!tech directory of their server, or in your own PSA system. That way, you can make sure that you do a thorough job each time.

The problem with this approach is that you might not touch every machine.

Therefore, you should have a policy to check updates on all machines on a regular basis. For servers, this is part of the regular monthly maintenance. Whether performed remotely or onsite, all updates will be applied at least once a month. For desktops, you will need to create a service request to update all machines. I recommend one service request per client (not one per machine). You will need to have a document for keeping track of which machines have been completed.

You should go through this process at least once a year. Ideally, you will do it once per quarter. You can see why an RMM tool can save you a LOT of time. These "sweeps" can be extremely time consuming if you manage a lot of machines. If you have an RMM tool, you can apply updates weekly or monthly with almost zero additional effort.

Automated Patch Management

Automated patch management is a life saver for managed service providers. If you have a thousand desktops and 100 servers, patching them adequately would be a full time job. The more you can automate the better.

The key with automated patch management is to decide how much you want to be involved. You can simply pass things through (e.g., If Microsoft released it, install it.). Or you can test each patch for yourself. Here's the process we follow:

1. Patch is released by Microsoft (Tuesday)

2. One business day later we look to see whether the patch has been recalled

3. We deploy the patch to our internal servers/workstations

4. Three-five business days later (assuming no problems), we deploy to client servers/workstations

If your RMM company has a patch approval feature, you could simply set up groups so that patches are deployed once they have been white listed. In this way, you simply rely on your RMM vendor to do the vetting for you.

Blacklisting Patches

For a variety of reasons, you might choose to blacklist some patches so they do not get installed. Sometimes this is applied throughout all your clients (for example, if there's a Microsoft patch that just causes problems). More commonly, you might have a specific customer's Line of Business (LOB) application that is incompatible with a specific patch or service pack.

Patches have three possible statuses: Pending Approval, Approved, and Denied.

When patches are denied, you need to be very certain that they do not get applied. That means you need to have strict policies in-house to make sure that everyone respects the "denied" status.

Interestingly enough, the "update" that is most likely to cause problems with client LOBs and web-based applications is Internet Explorer. How many times have we seen something break because a newer version of IE is installed? While I don't recommend avoiding all IE updates, please treat them with respect and be careful.

A Few Final Notes

Desktops can always be fixed, and don't normally affect the entire company. Servers are much more critical. Servers should always be backed up before patches are applied. Whether manual or automatic, stop the process until you have a good backup. I know things almost never go wrong with "simple" patches, but they sometimes DO go wrong. You need a way back without wasting a lot of (down)time.

As a general rule, the RMM company's patch approval process is probably good enough to rely on. But you know your clients and their computers better than anyone. You need to decide on a patch management level that makes sense and is comfortable for you.

You need to articulate that philosophy and make sure your staff understands it.

Three Take-Aways from This Chapter:

1. Don't just let patch installations "happen." Have a philosophy – *your* approach to how patches are installed. Write it down.

2. Define your process. Whatever it is, implement it consistently.

3. Create a blacklist policy. Even if you only have a few clients who need to blacklist patches, there might be a lot of work involved in ignoring this.

Three Action Steps for Your Company:

1. _____

_____

2. _____

_____

3. _____

_____

15

Setting Up Alerts in Your PSA and RMM

In the "old days" we got started in the monitoring business with the simple process I describe in the book *Service Agreements for SMB Consultants*. Basically, it consisted of a combination of server alerts emailed from Small Business Server and pages (text messages) sent from a product called Servers Alive. See www.woodstone.nu/salive. It's not very full-featured, but it kept us informed of the most import things – like server reboots!

Today, we have a PSA (professional services administration) tool and an RMM (remote monitoring and management) tool and can do a great deal more for our business. If you own these tools and are not using their alert features, today is a great day to start!

Many Kinds of Alerts

Like anything else, you don't want to get carried away with alerts, spamming yourself with emails and text messages. The goal, after all, is to make your entire operation run more smoothly and to keep your clients' systems operating at peak efficiency. So be judicious.

There are several kinds of monitoring. The most obvious type is done by the RMM. When disc space usage exceeds X%, an alert can be triggered. If you set it up right, you can have alerts automatically create tickets in your RMM system or in your PSA system.

But perhaps the most important part of your alert system is still the human side. You need a filter with some common sense. You also need to consider how to respond to different kinds of alerts. They're not all equal, you know.

RMM Alerts are the most obvious. A server reboots unexpectedly. A critical service stops. CPU usage is too high. When you look at your RMM tool, you should see lots of green lights and not very many red lights. And there are some red lights that just aren't very important.

The first thing you should do is look at your Monitoring Sets to see what you can easily monitor AND you want to know about. With some systems, you can get an alert every time a problem happens, but you get no notice when the problem goes away. That can leave technicians looking at issues that aren't really issues anymore. Even if you get notices that an alert has been cleared, you have to match up the Service Start and Service Stop notices.

So pick your alerts very carefully. One of the most common complaints about any new RMM system is that they are overwhelming. As a result, some people turn off all the alerts. Let's not go that far! This is a key feature. You do need to control the alerts, but don't eliminate them altogether.

I recommend you start slow. Pick a few key alerts and see how many emails or tickets you get. Obviously you want to monitor "Server Down" incidents. And probably Critical Impact issues.

But you probably do NOT want constant alerts if CPU usage is out of control on a server. You want that to show up on your board. You might even want it to create a ticket. But an issue like that can drag on a long time until it's fixed. You need to manage this kind of alert or you create a situation like the boy who cried wolf. Too many alerts will cause you and your techs to stop paying attention to alerts.

Some RMMs are extremely complicated and they want to charge you huge amounts of money to just do it for you. It makes you wonder why they didn't configure it correctly out of the box. Relax. Go slow. Educate yourself. And don't get overwhelmed.

Go slow. But start monitoring the most important stuff as soon as you can.

PSA alerts are a bit different. Basically, these consist of notifications that you have new service tickets. Here, management consists of handling each ticket appropriately. If tickets are automatically created by the RMM system, you need to be aware that cranking up monitoring will also crank up the tickets. Please see Chapters Eight and Eleven.

You need to have a human look at these regularly to make sure you don't have duplicate tickets, and that all tickets have the right priority. And whether you do it yourself or have a service coordinator, someone needs to make sure that all tickets are properly addressed and worked from highest priority to lowest priority, and from oldest to newest.

Just as with the RMM system, you have to decide: Do you want an email or text message every time a new ticket goes in the system? The answer is probably yes if you're very small OR you have your alerts under control. The longer machines are on managed service, the smoother they run and the fewer alerts they generate. So you may want to revisit this decision from time to time.

If you are just getting started with a PSA and RMM system, you will be overwhelmed. You'll be overwhelmed with how much you need to learn, with fine-tuning the system, and with alerts you've set up. At the beginning, crank the alerts way down. Don't panic. Your client systems are no worse off than before. You just know about all the little things you didn't know before!

In the big picture, you probably want the RMM to create certain kinds of service requests. All the "little" stuff can be on the monitoring board and get looked at once a day (see Chapter Thirteen). But the big stuff needs to be a high-priority or emergency ticket and you need to get a text message.

It might take you several attempts to get the balance right. Some computer alerts show up as "yellow" in the event logs, but they are critical to the network's health – like a failed backup. Others show up as "red" alerts because a service stopped, but it's a service you don't really use, such as synchronizing Exchange servers when you only have one.

I have worked with several coaching clients who turned up their alerts and became overwhelmed. So they turned it off, took months to clean up their service board, and didn't want to turn it on again. Unfortunately, this is very common.

If you're new to this process, commit to the process. Know that you will need to fine-tune. Turn it on for one day. Then tune it and turn it on for a week. Tune and fine-tune until you get it right.

Hours of operation

How you handle alerts should also vary based on time of day. You should have a written procedure for what happens when alerts come in after hours. We talk about our *Server Down Procedure* in Chapter

Seventeen, for example. But you should also have a general after-hours procedure.

I'm assuming that your managed service contract says that all work after 5:00 PM is not covered. You still need to keep an eye on the boards and massage service requests so they are in the right categories when the sun comes up. But if you only have a few low-level alerts, you can just look at the emails on your phone and determine that you don't have to log on and massage the board every hour of every day.

Other than Server Down situations, there's no reason to hang out on your service board looking for things to do. Relax. Enjoy your family. Go to work when the sun comes up.

Forms

There are no specific forms for implementing this SOP. You might write up a brief description of the procedures for RMM and PSA monitoring and put them into your SOP binder.

This kind of policy requires that everyone on the team

1) Be aware of the policy

2) Practice the policy

3) Correct one another's errors

4) Support one another with reminders

Three Take-Aways from This Chapter:

1. Evaluate the level of alerts you want to receive. Revisit this from time to time. Balance "enough" with too much.

2. Once you have a good alert system in place, relax and let the system do its job. Spend time with your family.

3. Let the RMM create service tickets. Then adjust the volume until it's just right for your company process.

Three Action Steps for Your Company:

1. _____

   _____

2. _____

   _____

3. _____

   _____

16

New PC Checklists

We've all had the "nightmare install" of a new computer. Everything should just work, but it doesn't. Everything should be smooth, but it isn't. Everything seems to be working now . . . until you drive away.

There are few example of Standard Operating Procedures (SOPs) that are more important to an I.T. consultant than the New PC Checklist. If you want to set up every machine the same way, no matter which tech does the work, and have a "perfect" install each time, you need a New PC Checklist.

Let's take a look.

Overview

A "New PC Checklist" is just what is sounds like: A checklist for setting up a new computer at a client office. If you don't have one, start today!!!

Setting up new computers is a very common thing in any business. Whether it's a new PC or moving people to new workstations, you need to make sure the hardware and software is set up so your client can sit down and just start working.

You have a certain way that you want machines set up. So do I. The chances that they're the same is about . . . 00.000001%. There are too many variables. Even within your office, different technicians will set up machines differently.

This is bad for several reasons. **Uniformity (consistency) always means greater efficiency.** Even doing setup tasks in a different order can increase the time needed to complete the job. Many clients have strange requirements (like a specific combination of patch levels) that need to be maintained.

In addition, of course, every client has a unique set of requirements. One client uses Adobe Acrobat; another uses PDF Complete. Some clients map all printers for all users; others map specific printers for each department. And so forth.

Benefits

Checklists also have the following benefits:

Sharing work.

One of the great benefits of any checklist is the ability to put down a job and then hand it off to someone else. One person can start a job at 4 PM and another can pick it up at 8 AM without duplicating work, forgetting anything, or having to start over. This makes it easy to hire temporary assistants from the local I.T. Pro user group. Yes, they could set up a computer "their" way. But with a checklist, they can now set it up YOUR way.

Guarantee that everything gets done.

As small as this sounds, it is critically important. Did you remove all the "free" junkware that shipped with the computer? Did you install the Adobe Reader? Did you remember the shared printer for the label-maker on Josie's workstation?

Guarantee that everything is done in the correct order.

Almost as important as the last point: It can make a huge difference to perform tasks in a specific order. For example, we like to keep machines disconnected from the network until fairly late in the process. That allows us to install all the software before we install the anti-virus. Few things will slow down an install more than a virus scan. Plus, of course, some software works best if you know the optimal order of installation so that newer .dll files don't get replaced by older files due to a poorly-behaved installation program.

You can handle more clients because you don't have to remember the peculiar setup of each one.

Huge. Once you have a template checklist for each client, you can free up your brain cells to work on other things. Knowing that you can just print off a checklist and knock out an installation for any client is a very powerful tool to have in your tool belt.

The bottom line: Consistency. Consistency means profit.

Without a checklist, even you will set up a machine differently every time. The client has no hope.

Implementation Notes

First, you need a master New PC Checklist. This will probably be 3-4 pages long, depending on how detailed you are. The master should be good enough to guarantee a good, clean installation on most new (or existing) clients. After all, 90% of what you and I do is the same. It's how we do it, the order in which we do it, and the peculiarities of the specific job that make the difference.

Second, you will create a unique New PC Checklist for each client. The client-specific checklists will include their IP address range, their printer configurations, their software products, and so forth. These lists should be stored on your server, either on your sky drive, SharePoint, or wherever your company stores files for technicians to access. You can keep a copy at the client site, but "the" master file for each client should be on your server. This is primarily for consistency, but is also handy when you make a change across all lists (clients).

Third, when you start a new installation, the first thing you will do is to read through and make corrections to the New PC Checklist. This is true whether you're setting up one machine or 25. Have you revved from Windows 7 to W8? Is there a newer procedure for the anti-virus? Did the client environment change in some way that affects workstations?

Fourth, if you are setting up more than one machine, you should execute the (revised) New PC Checklist as you set up one machine. That allows you to make notes about all updates and changes. Then you can update the master New PC Checklist for that client and run off copies for each new machine.

Fifth, you print out this checklist and tape it to each machine. At that time, you enter the machine name on the New PC Checklist. This guarantees that there's only one checklist per machine, and you know exactly where it is. Whoever sits down at that machine can begin at the beginning or pick up where someone left off.

Side Note: Using a Checklist

As strange as it sounds, you need to agree on ONE WAY to use a checklist. You'd be surprised what people come up with. Here's what I recommend:

1) Read the task

2) Execute the task

3) Check the box

I know, I know. What else would you do? But I'm telling you: people are clever. They come up with all kinds of ways to do this wrong.

- The worst offenders are those who go through three or four steps and then check the boxes.

- The worst offenders are people who "know what they're doing" and execute steps out of order.

- The worst offenders are those who sit down, check all the boxes, and then proceed to execute the steps.

See what I mean? The worst offenders are those who want to go fast and NOT follow the process. The process exists for a reason. Trust the process. Love the process. Use the process. The process is your friend. The process will make you rich!

Sixth, if you're working in a team, someone will be the "clean up" expert who tackles the weird stuff that comes up (even though it never should). That person must be able to sit down at any machine in the office and know for an absolute fact what has been done and what has not been done. They may need to back-track a bit. But they will know exactly where they are in the process.

And when that person is not killing monsters, they'll need to be able to jump in as just another technician . . . and pick up exactly where someone else left off.

Seventh, you'll take notes as you go along so you can update the checklist. It's amazing how fast things change. After only 30 days, you'll find that something's different. Windows, Office, anti-virus, Internet settings, spam filter, … something. So you'll update the checklist and load the update onto your server.

PLEASE don't put this off. You're there. You're in the middle of it. Your mind is fresh. And right now, today, it's billable. If you wait a day or two, your notes may be less useful. And you might feel bad about charging for it. Just do it. Make a little, save the client some money in the long run, and make yourself more profit in the long run. Just do it.

Forms

The basic form for this is one you probably have in your head. You can begin creating a new one by simply use a Trouble Shooting and Repair log (see Volume Three, Chapter Thirty). You can also use a blank writing tablet.

Simply write down every single thing you do. Remove the PC from the box. Make sure the cards and memory are tight. Plug into UPS. Etc.

Every little detail.

Wherever you skip specific details, the technician will do whatever makes sense at the moment. Sometimes that's fine. Sometimes is adds an hour to the job, which costs you money.

Once complete, begin using the checklist per the instructions above. Ideally, every technician will have the skills and common sense to improve the checklist every time it's used. Once you put this process in place, it is self-perpetuating because the last item on the checklist is Update the checklist!

Of course I've included a sample New PC Checklist in with the downloadable material that you receive with this book. But that's just the start – you need to customize it for each client.

This kind of policy requires that everyone on the team

1) Be aware of the policy

2) Practice the policy

3) Correct one another's errors

4) Support one another with reminders

Three Take-Aways from This Chapter:

1. If you want to set up every machine the same way, no matter which tech does the work, and have a "perfect" install each time, you need a New PC Checklist.

2. Uniformity (consistency) always means greater efficiency.

3. Define a "model" New PC Checklist and then create custom checklists for each client environment.

Three Action Steps for Your Company:

1. _____

   _____

2. _____

   _____

3. _____

   _____

17

Server Down Procedures

There's a fun meme going around Facebook about "What I Really Do." That set of juxtapositions is humorous because it's got some grain of truth to it. What my Mother thinks I do . . . Why my friends think I do . . . What my customers think I do . . . and so forth.

Taking care of servers is a little bit like that. What the customer thinks you do, and what other technicians think you do may not be at all what you really do.

I am adamant that we don't work evenings and weekends. But many people who haven't tried that are skeptical. Very often, techs challenge me during presentations. "Well what happens when the server goes down? You have to work evenings and weekends. You have to stop everything and work on that. You can't schedule your time. You can't plan these things. You're stuck until the server's up."

The day I realized that NONE of that is true, my business became suddenly more successful.

Mini Rant on Server Downtime

First, Servers don't fail.

If your business consists of putting out fires and doing break-fix work on servers YOU sold, built, and maintain, then you're in the wrong business. Either you're selling the wrong server, putting it together wrong, or maintaining it wrong.

Servers don't fail. Servers run and run and run.

What's the wrong server to sell? One that's already out of date, technologically. One that that's underpowered when it's new. One that's a cheap piece of crap you've upgraded to "server level." One that you've packed with cheap parts and third party add-ons instead of manufacturer approved parts. One you built yourself with individual parts.

We sell HP business class servers. The ML 350 is the workhorse. On average, these servers run three to five years with ZERO issues of any kind.

Maintenance is a no-brainer today. Use GFI Max, Continuum, LabTech or some other RMM tool. Get a tool that monitors everything you do, reports issues, and allows you to patch the system remotely for every single client while you sleep. Do regularly scheduled monthly maintenance. Test your backups. Tune up machines. Love them and they will treat you well.

Many people don't believe me. Mike didn't believe me when he came to work for me. "How is it possible that you never have a server failure?" Now he sells them, builds them, maintains them the right way. And they never fail. Period.

Second, You never have to work evenings and weekends unless YOU choose to.

We have a simple policy: Work during the hours 5:00 PM and 8:00 AM is not covered by managed service and is twice our regular service rate. All weekend and holiday work is also twice the price.

So . . . fixing a critical issue during business hours is covered by managed services. At 5:01 PM we go to $300 per hour and we burn at that rate until the system is fixed or the client sends us home. In almost every case, the client sends us home.

If the client chooses to have us work all night at $300/hr, we are happy to do that.

Third, Even critical labor is scheduled and planned.

When your heater goes out during the first freeze of the year, or your air conditioner goes out the first time it hits 100 degrees outside, you have a crisis. And you call the repair place. And what do they say? "We'll get there as soon as we can."

Servers are the same way. You want to calmly come to a stopping point with other projects. You want to put everything in a nice orderly state so you can go work on the server. It might take you an hour to calmly put things in order so you can go address the critical issue and give it your full attention.

Panic serves no one. It doesn't serve the client you're leaving behind and it doesn't serve the client you're going to.

TALK to your client. Don't assume downtime is the end of the world. Let them know that you will be there and give them an idea of when. You can only do what you can do.

Important safety tip for life: You CAN prepare for emergencies. You CAN have a standard operating procedure for when servers go down. You don't have to panic. You don't have to act like this has never happened before. You don't have to make bad decisions because you're in a hurry.

You can have a rational, calm, profitable response to an emergency.

[End of Rant]

Okay. Having said all that, there are weird instances when something goes wrong on a server.

But it's the exception to the norm. You can't build your business around something that almost never happens. Build your business around the standard processes that happen every single day. Make that profitable.

Then build a process around "emergencies" that is also profitable.

Define a Priority One Incident

I have mentioned the priority system and how you set priorities on several occasions. See Chapters Seven and Eight.

Priority One issues are never set by a human being. They set themselves. A fire, a flood, a failed hard drive, a motherboard failure. That sort of thing.

I hope you're saying, "Hard drive is a bad example. We have redundancy. No single hard drive failure can bring down a business." Yes. That's true if you sold the right server, built the server, and maintain it properly. If you inherited the server from Cousin Larry's Pretty Good I.T. Shop, then your server is down.

Anyway, Priority One means Critical. A P1 sets itself. That means

- Server down
- Network down

- Email System down

- Server based Line of Business application down

- Fire, flood, earthquake, hazmat spill, etc.

A server down situation is considered any outage of a server or major LOB (line of business) services such as Exchange or SQL that is not planned. At times, especially over the weekend, a server might reboot due to patch management. As long as the RMM (remote monitoring and management) tool reports that the server is back up in a reasonable amount of time, you may safely ignore the issue during off hours. You'll still want to look and verify that it was "normal" the next business day.

Server Down During Normal Business Hours

The normal process for working service requests is from highest priority to lowest priority, and from oldest to newest. So all P1s are more important than all P2s, and older P1s are more important than newer P1s.

You should almost never have a P1 in your system. So when it happens, it needs serious attention.

In the normal course of your day, you'll be working on something else when a P1 comes in. Whoever manages the service board needs to acknowledge the client in a timely manner. If it is after 3:00 PM, be sure to let the client know that all work up until 5PM is covered and all work after that is at the after-hours rate.

The service coordinator (I know these all might be the same person) needs to decide who should work the ticket. In most SMB shops this is going to be the owner/tech or the lead tech. That person is doing something else right now. So you need to coordinate having the current job come to an orderly stop or have someone else take over.

You can't leave one paying client to go to another without taking care of the first client. They'll understand that someone has a server down. But you still need to leave their business in an orderly state.

Note: It is critical that everyone on the team constantly check to make sure 1) Tickets are in the right Queue (or service board); 2) Tickets are assigned the correct Priority Level; 3) Tickets have the right service agreement attached to them; and 4) Work type and sub-type are correct (e.g., maintenance vs. add/move/change). If you all check these things constantly for every ticket, then managing workflow around a critical issue will be easier.

If you can connect remotely and work on the issue, you should do this. Remote work provides a faster response and may allow you to solve the issue without a trip. If you have an ILO (integrated lights out, or equivalent) card installed and activated, you can get to the console level on the server even if the operating system won't load. That allows you to run hardware level diagnostics and updates as well as access the operating system in active directory restore mode. This gets back to selling the right server.

Once you begin working on the P1 ticket, nothing takes higher priority. The only thing that might be more important is an older P1.

Once a P1 is in progress, the Status Update becomes critical. See Chapter Six. Your client might never read their monthly reports or invoices. But after a server down situation, they just might want to discuss response time and performance.

So, the ticket moves from New to Acknowledged. Then to Assigned, and probably to Work in Progress (skipping Schedule This and Scheduled).

Once the work is in progress, it will stay there until one of three things happens. First, you fix the problem. This includes a temporary fix that puts the client back in business. You'll close out the P1 and create a P3 ticket to order parts, update software, etc. That properly puts an end to the crisis and moves work to a schedule status.

Second, if the client is not willing to pay for after-hours work, then a ticket will move to "Scheduled" for 8:00 AM the next business day. Yes this does happen.

Third, in the process of fixing the issue, you need to wait for a third party vendor (for software, hardware, network, etc.), then the status goes to Waiting Materials, Waiting Results, or Waiting Vendor.

There are other weird things that happen, but you don't have to have SOPs for things that you can't foresee. So the client might decide in the middle of all this to buy a new server, put the project on hold until he has more money, or something else. Again, weird stuff you don't expect.

Server Down During Off Hours Procedure

The procedure for after-hours support has mostly to do with processing the alert so you can execute essentially the same response you would have during business hours.

First, determine what constitutes business hours. For us it's Monday through Friday 8am to 5pm. And we all know that there are "golden hours" of 7-8 AM and 5-6 PM when we might do a little work at standard rates. But that normally happens for scheduled work, not for emergency response.

We assume that you have some kind of system to alert you when a server goes down. You get a text message. You get an email. A technician in India calls your cell phone. Something.

Note: If a server goes down outside of working hours, your company will know about it before the client does. If you have more than one technician, your techs need to really use your PSA system (e.g., Autotask, ConnectWise, TigerPaw) to communicate with one another. That means accurate status updates and notes.

Second, Tech notes are always critical. Keep track of every single thing you tried, the order in which you did things, what you observed, and the time for everything. If you need to call escalated support (Microsoft, HP, Dell, Third Tier, Dove Help Desk, etc.), the more information you have the better.

If for any reason you do not have access to the PSA system, you must take very good notes for when you do have access. You are expected to update the PSA as soon as possible. For now, we assume you do have access to the PSA.

Third, monitor the system and determine whether it's P1. Is the server just rebooting? How do you know? Create the service ticket. You can create a P1 even if it later gets changed to P3. But if you haven't scheduled a reboot, then it's a legitimate P1.

Fourth, Perform the client call down process in the event of a server down.

You should have a note in your PSA about the client call down. Every one of your clients should fill out a simple form that says who should be called first, second, and third. You should have first, second, and (if you can) third phone numbers for each contact.

If you have an alarm system, this is very similar to the form they use. If you do not have access to the required contact phone numbers for whatever reason, you must contact anyone inside your company who can get them for you.

Call Down Procedure:

1) Go to the Company page in your PSA system and look under the section "After Hours Contacts." Start by calling the primary contact and then work your way down the list.

2) If you reach a voice mail box (including the company's general mailbox) the recommended script is as follows:

"Hello this is [insert technician name here] calling from [your company]. We have received a page alerting us that the server [insert server name here] is currently unreachable. This is not a planned outage and we have created a priority one service request. This call is just to inform you of the current status. We will call back with further updates. Our normal hours of operation are Monday through Friday, 8am to 5pm and we will begin working on the issue during those hours."

3) If you reach a person, convey all of the same information above. In addition, you must ask them if they would like us to begin working on the issue outside of normal business hours. Script:

"As the primary contact, do you wish to authorize off-hours work to be performed for this issue? Off-hours work is not covered under managed services and would be billed out at double rate." (typically $300 / hour)

IF YES:

Inform the contact that the service request has been assigned a Priority 1, a technician will be assigned, and they will begin working on the issue as soon as possible. That technician will be contacting you and might require access to the site. If so please be prepared to have someone meet our tech at the location.

IF NO:

> Inform the contact that the service request has been assigned a
> Priority 1 and we will begin working on the issue as soon as our
> office opens. Answer any questions and then conclude the call by
> reaffirming that we will call again if the status changes.

4) If you can only reach the secondary contact, be aware that the
   secondary contact may NOT be able to authorize off-hours
   billable work. Anyone Authorized to incur after-hours labor
   expenses should be noted in the PSA system with an (A) next to
   their name.

Misc. Notes

In Volume Three, Chapter Nine of this series we discussed managing
after-hours technicians and the service coordinator. In many cases,
the person hired to catch calls after hours is NOT authorized to begin
executing the work. In particular with a server, the person who
catches the alert might not be qualified to work the ticket.

Make sure that part of your process for the after-hours tech is to
know whether or not they are authorized to begin working a ticket. If
not, then you need a call-down for your own technicians to find
someone who is authorized.

Any service request that requires third party vendors who are not
available should be set to the status of "Waiting on Vendor." Make
sure your notes are up to date! In a perfect world, the vendor will
arrange a time to start working on the system. Ha ha. I know.
Anyway, you might not be the one working the issue when the
vendor calls, so perfect notes are required.

Implementation

There are several pieces to this that you should already have in place.

You need a definition of Priorities. See Chapter Seven.

You need a definition of Statuses. See Chapter Six.

You need a policy about hourly rates, when they're applied, etc.

You need to create a call-down form and have each of your clients fill it out. This could be an online form. This information should be stored in your PSA system and available to the after-hours tech/service coordinator.

You absolutely CAN prepare for emergencies. Most of the preparation consists of having processes in place before the crisis hits. Your team needs to know how to massage the service board, how to set priorities and adjust work types, etc. Once everyone on your team gets in the habit of touching all these bases on a regular basis, then a P1 is just another process to execute.

Three Take-Aways from This Chapter:

1. Create a call-down list for every client. Ideally, you want three phone number each for three people for each company.

2. Create a "skills matrix" or otherwise determine who is authorized to work emergency tickets after hours.

3. If you live in an environment where servers fail frequently, take time to examine why this is happening. This is a serious issue that reflects a much larger problem.

Three Action Steps for Your Company:

1. _____

_____

2. _____

_____

3. _____

_____

18

Third Party Tech Support - Documenting Calls

In the next chapter we'll talk about the "Rules of Engagement" for third party tech support. In this chapter we'll cover documentation related to third party support.

One of the key tools you need is the *Troubleshooting and Repair Log* described in Volume Three, Chapter Thirty. This is a paper log so you can keep it on your desk and add notes very easily as needed. At some point you might scan this into your PSA system (Autotask, ConnectWise, TigerPaw, etc.), or transcribe some of the highlights.

Documentation is Critical

There are several pieces to documenting an outbound tech support call. First, you need to get all the relevant information into your PSA system. This includes information on the vendor, their contact information, SR(x) numbers, service contract information, etc. You need all this in the PSA, within a specific ticket, so that all time can be logged to this ticket. Having everything in the PSA also allows you to have more than one technician on your staff work on the issue, and for you to put the project down and pick it up again.

Second, you need the paper TSR Log mentioned above. Please read that chapter! I can already hear people whining that everything should be electronic and not paper, blah, blah, blah. But it is just not practical to think that you will keep a service ticket open all the time, on a portable device, and keep that device in your hand at all times while working on this service call. It might be ten hours. It might be three days!

You need to be able to have instant random access to this document. This is true in large part because you have to coordinate with the other tech team. So you might need to add something to that document while you're between clients, at home, when the Internet is down, while the client's systems are offline, etc. Paper works anywhere, 100% of the time.

In a perfect world, everything is 100% electronic instantly. But many people are doing little or no documentation now, so the argument about waiting for an electronic option just doesn't float. Something is better than nothing.

Of course you will transfer some highlights from the TSR Log into the ticketing system when appropriate.

Third, you need to have some standard processes for describing how you deal with vendors. See the next chapter. Also, you should have at least one ticket status specifically for vendors. Because there just aren't that many vendor calls, I would not create a whole series of statuses. One - "Waiting on Vendor" - should suffice. But you need to be very good about documenting WHY you're waiting.

Sometimes, with 3rd party support, you need to arrange a specific time when they can get into the client's system. You need to inform the client, arrange the time, and have one of your technicians available for the call.

Because you'll be shadowing the vendor (or they'll be shadowing you) most of the time, coordinating multiple connections can be hassle. Keep good notes and make sure time gets allocated to the right service ticket.

If you do this consistently, you'll be able to figure out how much time you spent on each vendor at the end of the year. For example, if all calls to Symantec go into service requests specific to their products, then you can just add up the hours.

Working with vendors can be very time-consuming. There is often a long wind-up to getting funneled to someone who can actually help. You need to coordinate access to machines. If they end up sending a part for you to install – or a tech to install it – there's more coordination. Then, in the middle of your support cycle, someone needs a day off. Or you need to wait three days to see if the fix worked. It can be very time-consuming, and you need to document everything.

Reproducible Success

One of the most powerful elements of documenting your calls with tech support is the ability to get a free education! Once you are involved in solving an issue, you may very well be able to fix it by yourself next time. The odds of success go way up when you take excellent notes.

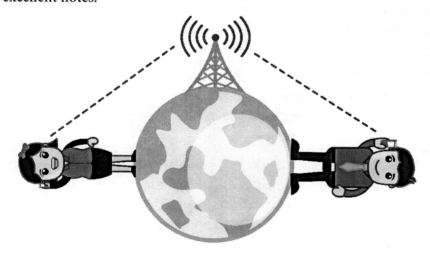

In all of the sample cases discussed in the next chapter, YOU need to keep great notes about what you did. You need time stamps for all activities, in 15 minute increments.

It can save a lot of time if you can tell the escalated support what you've already done. This includes backtracking your steps (for example, when you change an IP, test something, change the IP back to what it was). Tell them everything.

If you can email your notes to the tech, that sometimes helps tremendously. Keeping excellent notes will help you escalate to the right level of support as quickly as possible. You always want to be working with someone who is more knowledgeable than you.

When the third party takes over, you also need to keep notes on everything they do. Very often, these people write up their notes after the fact. In other words, they don't document in real time. That means you will be relying on their perfect recall, which they won't have.

You need to log emails and get them into the ticket notes.

If the "fix" is related to a product that you have installed on more than one client, you need to make sure that notes get into the knowledgebase you keep for that product. If you're not doing this in your PSA system, learn how and do it!

No matter which third party vendor you're dealing with, ask for their notes and put them into your service ticket or knowledgebase. This is critical for documenting what you did and might help with future problems.

There's one very frustrating category of problems you can't solve yourself: Secret patches. Nothing is more irritating than to have someone on a paid support call say "We only distribute this patch to people who ask for it." What? So after an hour of scouring your online database, you tell me I would never have found this without calling you? Grrrrr.

But even with this, you can download the patch, document how you used it, and have it available as needed.

As I mentioned, you probably don't have THAT many 3rd party support calls. If you have a high number for one product, you should consider alternative products! But because you don't have a lot, you'll need to have good processes in place so that you can deal with them as successfully and consistently as possible.

Three Take-Aways from This Chapter:

1. Re-dedicate to using TSR Logs. Use one on every Priority One ticket and every time you deal with third party tech support.

2. To the extent possible, take control of the communication with the third party tech. Arrange for them to connect when it's easiest for you to have multiple techs on hand.

3. Keep up with your notes. With a small effort to keep up, you will have better notes than any vendor support line you talk to.

Three Action Steps for Your Company:

1. _____

   _____

2. _____

   _____

3. _____

   _____

19

Third Party Tech Support - Rules of Engagement

From time to time, you need to call third party tech support. That means HP, Dell, Microsoft, Symantec, etc. It also includes line of business vendors, ISPs, and other folks who are hired by your clients.

You need to have policies regarding third party support for a number of reasons. First, you need to have consistent communications with outside parties. Second, you need to log all time appropriately. Third, you need to manage the vendor relationship. And, fourth, you need to protect the client systems.

As with so many policies, these come from a series of experiences in the "real world."

Over the years I've been amazed how good some of the vendor tech support is. Of course there are exceptions. But many of them are excellent. So you have to judge very quickly whether you have a "good one" on the phone.

Let's assume that most of the vendors you're working with are large, have good processes, and have competent technicians. Again, everyone has stories about bad support, but I'm amazed at how rare that is.

In this chapter, our focus is on how to maximize performance and documentation when it comes to third party tech support.

You will generally have three types of vendor interactions. One is a direct relationship with your company. For example, you call tech support for equipment you own internally. A second is contacting a company on behalf of your client regarding a very standardized installation such as an operating system or backup software. And a third type involves a company that makes customized software tuned to your client's environment, such as a Line of Business application (LOB).

1. Internal to Your Company

For the "internal" vendor relationship, you need to keep track of contact information, account numbers, telephone numbers, and the standard information you need with any vendor. This information is best kept in your PSA system (Autotask, ConnectWise, TigerPaw, etc.).

Your policy for direct vendor relationships should state very clearly who may contact the vendor, and who may authorize contact with the vendor. This is particularly important if you are paying for support, such as with an escalated tech support provider such as Third Tier or Dove Help Desk. If it costs you money to use the service, then there needs to be a clear chain of command about who can make the decision to engage, and how you will proceed.

All time spent dealing directly with vendors for your company must be logged as administrative time or internal support time. You need to track for payroll purposes, but you also need to be able to run reports and determine how many hours it takes to work with a given vendor in a year. If a vendor costs you a significant amount of time in a year, it might be worth looking for another vendor. Or, at a minimum, building them into your budget for the next year.

You need to have an escalation policy. For example, if the third party tech works for an hour without making forward progress, then you request escalation. This requires excellent notes on your part. Many companies, including Microsoft and Continuum, resist escalation at all costs. Hold firm to your policies.

2. Standard-Install Software or Operating System

For standard-install software at a client site, you just need to keep all the information within that client's section of your PSA. With these standard install kinds of software, you can expect to get a different technician every time. The vendor will generally NOT have any kind of account on the client's computer system. You will probably be working on a ticket when you decide to escalate for support.

In such cases, you have to decide whether to continue logging time on the current service ticket or create a new one. This is mostly a matter of personal preference, but it can be very handy to create a separate ticket for the escalated support if you think it will take a significant amount of time. It's sometimes hard to distinguish how much time was spent on the escalated part of a ticket. But if you have a separate ticket, it's easy.

Whenever working with a third-party support team, we prefer to do the work ourselves and not let them work directly on client machines. But sometimes it's their policy to work directly, or it just makes sense. When that happens, we allow them to shadow us. We do not let them have access to client systems when we are not monitoring what they do. Our preference is for them to tell us what to do and have us make the changes.

They know their software, but we know our client machines.

When working with these vendors, remember that you'll often start out with someone who knows less than you. Unfortunately, no one knows that until you've spent some time going over familiar ground. See the comments on documentation and honesty below. If the tech knows less than you, then they're wasting time. Escalate as soon as possible. If you know less than them, sit back and take excellent notes.

Tracking time is critical. There are generally two types of time that can be used here. One is "covered" by managed services and therefore you are losing money. The other is billable to the client as part of a project or hourly job. In one case, you need to know exactly how long it took to fix a problem. In the other case, you need to be able to bill the client for exactly how long it took to fix the problem.

This requires the same policy as above: You need to have an escalation policy. For example, if the third party tech works for an hour without making forward progress, then you request escalation. This requires excellent notes on your part.

3. Customized Software or Line of Business

Unfortunately, this is the area where we run into the least "professional" tech support. Sometimes the Line of Business vendors are very much like standard-install software vendors. But just as often, it's a 1-5 person company and there's only one person who can really fix anything. He might be using old programming languages, and he might not know anything about newer protocols or operating systems.

You need to determine very quickly whether you know more than this person. Be honest (see below). And defend your client's systems.

Unlike the other types of third-party support, the customized programmer or LOB vendor will probably have an actual logon to the client's system. Here's how we handle this.

a) The vendor account is not an administrator unless it is absolutely necessary. Server Operator is probably good enough.

b) The vendor account is disabled at all times when you are not logged in and shadowing them.

c) The client must sign a release stating that your company is in charge of managing vendors. This reduces friction and makes it clear that you are in charge of the server.

d) If possible, the vendor will shadow you and you will do the work. But realistically, they will be much faster with their product than you, so you will probably end up shadowing them.

e) The vendor must walk you through what they're doing. You need to be attentive and make sure they don't make changes that will break something else.

f) All access to the server must be scheduled. You agree (normally by email) when the account will be activated. You coordinate a time when you can both access the server, and you keep great notes about what occurred. Some LOB vendors will send you their amazing notes. Most don't keep any notes.

Escalation may or may not be an option. If you got to the one guy who can actually fix stuff, you may need to just hang in there until he figures it out.

Documentation is Critical

In the last chapter we talked about Documenting Calls. But here are some key notes:

In all of these cases, YOU need to keep great notes about what you did. You need time stamps for all activities, in 15 minute increments.

It can save a lot of time if you can tell the escalated support what you've already done. This includes backtracking your steps (for example, when you change an IP, test something, change the IP back to what it was). Tell them everything.

Keeping excellent notes will help you escalate to the right level of support as quickly as possible. You always want to be working with someone who is more knowledgeable than you.

If the "fix" is related to a product that you have installed on more than one client, you need to make sure that notes get into the knowledgebase you keep for that product. If you're not doing this in your PSA system, learn how and do it!

Honesty is the Best Policy

When service companies reach a level of true professionalism, they adopt a policy of complete honesty in service calls. That means you admit if you or your client broke something. It doesn't mean you're incompetent. It means you're human. Expect the same from the vendor.

It's okay to say "I don't know about that." It's also okay to educate the vendor rep if you DO know something they don't. Be honest about what you did, the order in which you did it, and how you got where you are. Honesty is the fastest way to getting the system working again.

We all hate it when clients say "I didn't change anything," even when we can see that they installed a program. Don't be like that.

I've mentioned already, but let me say again: You always want to be working with someone who is more knowledgeable than you. That means you need to be honest about yourself. When you get to the limits of your knowledge, go into student mode and start soaking up new knowledge. When you get to the limits of the other technician's knowledge, ask to be escalated.

As always, excellent documentation is your friend.

Learn from Vendor Processes

Just as you have a service board, your vendors each have a service board. You need to document how you will contact them. For example, do you create a ticket online or by telephone? What information do they need?

One very common process that is used by tech support providers at all levels is to define the problem. You can't call a vendor and ask them to spend an hour poking around in your system and fine-tuning everything they find, unless you're paying them for it. No. In most cases, you have a specific problem. You called to fix that problem. They have a duty to define the problem, fix the problem, and close their service ticket.

If you also have another problem with the same software, expect it to be a separate service incident. In some cases, a tech will help you with both. But it is in everyone's interest to work on one problem at a time. So you are likely to have two different service tickets in their system.

Pay attention to processes like these and determine why they exist and how they serve you and the support company. Should you adopt similar policies? Very often, the answer is YES!

Implementing These Policies

Implementing these policies is a little different than other policies. You normally don't call a given tech support company very much. If you do, you might consider selling a different product! So you need to write up a policy that makes sense.

Only create as much policy as you need. When your staff need to escalate calls to outside vendors, go over these policies with them and use the incident to fine-tune your policies.

Especially with LOB vendors and customized software, you might have a specific policy for one vendor. Just make sure that there are clear notes about it in the system and that you have good communication internally, with the client, and with the vendor.

Always be updating documentation and processes.

Three Take-Aways from This Chapter:

1. You always want to be working with someone who is more knowledgeable than you. Monitor this. Be brutally honest.

2. Honesty is the fastest way to getting the system working again.

3. A good vendor support technician will want to define one problem very specifically and get your buy-in. Watch and learn. That's exactly what you should be doing in your company.

Three Action Steps for Your Company:

1. _____

  _____

2. _____

  _____

3. _____

  _____

20

Document Pouches

This Chapter is very practical in nature and geared toward the service delivery folks. It is a great procedure for client machines as well as your internal operations.

One of the best decisions I ever made in my business was to buy a number of the "pocket" file folders to store information about hardware and software. We use them to store all the information for a specific purchase. It is easy to set up a new folder when you are setting up a new computer.

It is a major pain in the neck and waste of time if you don't do this!

Let's start with an example. I recently bought a new video camera. The first thing I did was to grab one of these pouches and label it. Into the pouch goes the receipt, the warranty information, unused cables, and all the little paperwork you get with a new purchase. The folder is labeled and dated.

In this case, the instruction manual did not go in the pouch because I wanted to read it. Once that was accomplished, in it went.

I recommend that you adopt this policy for all machines you touch or manage internally and at each of your clients. There are many good reasons for this.

First, this is an easy way to keep all the information for that machine in one place. This includes add-ons such as documentation and warranty information for DVDs, sound cards, video cards, etc.

Second, this is a great place to make sure you keep track of all the stuff while you're building a machine.

Third, down the road when you want to know where you can find the factory re-installation discs, they are easy to find.

Fourth, if there's some kind of warranty issue, or software needs to be re-installed, you've got all the information in one place.

Fifth, in case of a fire, flood, or theft, you've got the information you need for an insurance claim.

Sixth, when it's time to send the machine to recycling, you can just send this pouch along with it. If you've been diligent at keeping up with this process, then everything related to that machine is in the pouch.

This collection of paperwork and software – plus the Machine Spec Sheet – will make for much faster service when needed.

The alternative is all too familiar to us: There's a junk drawer with unorganized discs and paperwork. It contains video and network drivers for all kinds of machines – most of which you don't own any more. And there are some missing because they were put in another drawer or not filed at all.

When I started my business, building machines yourself was a lot more common. So the most common place for "documentation" was the box that had shipped with the motherboard for the server. It was a handy size, held lots of paperwork, and was large enough for stray jumper wires and bits of hardware. But even those were normally out of date, included drivers and paperwork for machines that no longer existed, and had important software missing. Normally, the missing software was the thing you were actually looking for.

With the pouch system, you have one pouch for each machine and one pouch for important software packages. For example, if you have Microsoft Open licenses, you'll want to keep a good set of DVDs in the pouch along with the license certificates, license keys, etc. The same is true for Line of Business applications, multi-user QuickBooks or Business Works programs, etc.

Yes, a lot of this information is also electronic and is also in your PSA or on your company SharePoint site. But ALL of it should be in this pouch.

At the "end of life" for a given machine, you get rid of this file. That way, your filing system contains all the important files and software for everything you own, and none of the old files for equipment you no longer own.

You should dedicate a file drawer (or several) to these folders so that you can always find them quickly. Some clients put this information into paper file boxes and keep them on shelves next to the server. So you might have one file box for servers and network equipment and additional boxes for desktops and laptops.

Note that I mentioned network equipment. You will create files for routers, switches, firewalls, scanners, printers, label makers, shipping scales, etc. Everything that you touch that has warranty information, drivers, or software needs to be filed in a pouch.

The answer to the question "Where is the information on this ...?" should always be: In a pouch, where it belongs.

Everyone on your staff needs to get in the habit of making these file pouches with every new computer sale, every server build, every monitor delivery, and so forth. Just do it. 100% is easy to achieve. Make sure the creation of the pouch is part of the New PC Checklist.

And it's not a bad habit for your home equipment either.

The Big Bonus: This kind of standard operating procedure makes you look really good to your clients. Think about how many new clients you've taken on that had a simple system like this. It adds instant value and demonstrates that you know what you're doing. You do this a lot - and you've got a process for making everything easy.

Three Take-Aways from This Chapter:

1. Buy 10-20 "pocket" file folders and keep them on hand. You might add they to the technicians' scary box.

2. Develop a process for using these pouch folders and expect 100% compliance on day one.

3. Make sure that the creation of the pouch folders is written into the New PC build checklist, the New Server checklist, and every other New-Something checklist.

Three Action Steps for Your Company:

1. _____

_____

2. _____

_____

3. _____

_____

Section II –

Service Focus: Monthly Maintenance

21

Why We Do Monthly Maintenance

In the next six chapters we are going to do a deep-dive into a process that could be the central piece of your managed service business: Monthly Maintenance. I built my successful Managed Services business on this one core element.

Because I came from a world of mainframes and minis, with disc drives the size of two-drawer file cabinets, we did monthly maintenance. We did daily backups. We spent serious effort building systems that worked every day and could be relied on 100% of the time.

So when I went out into the wild as a technician, I simply assumed that we would do monthly maintenance. Even in the very early days, I made this part of my contracts. I did not include it for "free" back then. So I told clients that they needed to pay for monitoring and pay for monthly maintenance.

Regular Server Maintenance is the Core of Our Business

Way back when I started my first business (1995), I did what most consultants do: I figured it out. I took the knowledge I had and struck out on my own, in search of gold. I offered up "services" and waited for the phone to ring.

But the phone didn't ring. Apparently, the universe did not know that I'd spent $60 on business cards and I was now a consultant. So I had to go dig up my own clients (gold). That meant I needed a pitch. I needed a way to get my foot in the door.

If you've ever sold subscriptions of any kind, you know it's a one-two punch with a kicker. First, what am I giving away for free right now today? Second, what will you get if you sign up today and welcome me back every month? The answers to these questions make up your sales pitch. And the kicker is: If the prospect says no, what can I do to get invited back some day? Here's what I came up with.

First, I will give you a **free analysis** of your computer systems. Are they working right? Are they in good health? Are they making you money or costing you money? Note: My assumption was that I would never come across the perfect network. Therefore, everyone needs at least a little help. And, therefore, I would generate job proposals from every network analysis ever performed. This turned out to be true and is still true twenty years later.

Second, I propose to come back every month and **tune up** your server. I'll verify that you are properly protected, backed up, and virus scanned. I'll put in all the patches and fixes and updates. If you want, I'll even monitor your system remotely so that I get paged (it was 1995, remember) when something goes wrong. Most monthly maintenance is performed in about an hour. On rare occasions it takes longer. So the cost is about one hour of labor per month. Plus monitoring for $150/mo. Later I raised this to $250/mo to cover software costs, and about two hours labor. No complaints.

Kicker: If you really don't want monthly maintenance, may I please put you on my mailing list? We provide a monthly newsletter for free. Of course you can cancel any time.

And that's how it all began. Clients sometimes hired me to put out fires. But normally that was not my first contact. My first contact was to convince them to let me look at their computers. Nine times out of ten I found a snake pit of a network that had been neglected for years. So while I wasn't putting out a fire, I WAS solving a problem and increasing their performance. And I got invited back every month.

As you can imagine, in the days before "managed services" I found problems on a regular basis. Over time the server got better and better. But neglected desktops had problems. Old network equipment failed. Because I was onsite at least once a month, I was the computer guy for each of these offices. So I got all the calls.

But the server also got older. So eventually, performance degraded. When hard drives spin 24x7 for three years, they start to have issues. Bad sectors. Maybe a fan gets noisy. More and more software means less and less disc space, and longer backups. The maintenance never stops. But here's an important key to success: I entered the scene without recommending a new server (nine times out of ten). I did maintenance that pushed out the need for a new server. I was saving my clients money and they knew it.

At the same time, because I got to see them every month, I exposed them to my philosophies about computer maintenance, most of which you've seen in this 4-volume set.

> "We only quote and sell business class equipment."

> "Everything we sell has at least a one year warranty. We prefer three."

> "We like to see machines get replaced every three years."

> "A good server will give maximum performance for about three years."

"If you replace 1/3 of your computers each year, your costs will be very predictable and all of your equipment will always be under warranty."

This is like drip marketing. I might support a server for 2-3 years before I finally tell them that they need to get a new one. By that time they are fully indoctrinated into the "Karl way of thinking" about computers.

It is a great business policy, in my opinion, to help clients avoid big costs as long as possible. It's good for their wallets and good for your relationship. But when they DO need to buy something, it is also a good policy to tell them that they need to spend money. If you started the relationship by being frugal with the client's money and giving good long-term advice, you'll be very credible when it's time to recommend that they spend some of that money.

Welcome to Managed Services

Eventually, we had fifteen servers on a monthly maintenance schedule . . . at $250 each. This included all remote monitoring and monthly maintenance. It did NOT include labor to fix anything outside of the monthly maintenance visit. Therefore, basically everything was billable.

Eventually, I decided that I could use some of that money to buy RMM (remote monitoring and management) licenses. (By the way, that's when I joined ASCII because I saved so much money on licenses that it paid for my ASCII membership times ten. See www.ascii.com.) After that I had 100 RMM agents. I could monitor those 15 servers plus another 85!

Managed service allowed us to monitor desktops with the same attention we gave to servers. That meant we developed offerings to keep the entire office patched, fixed, and updated.

With managed services, we now do a lot more remotely. And because machines are monitored 24x7, almost all of the "check-ups" on the MMC (Monthly Maintenance Checklist) are handled automatically. For example, free disc space is now just an alert. When the light turns red or we get an RMM alert, a ticket is created. So we check the main portal every morning and handle any issues that arise.

All of that managed service activity gave the clients a better level of service than they ever had before. BUT it also meant that they see us a lot less. So we have to make a point of staying in touch and making sure the client knows us and loves us. Otherwise, everything works perfectly, but we don't get the credit!

Why We Do Monthly Maintenance

So, finally we get to the summary. We do monthly maintenance because:

1) It is central to our business that we lead the entire client relationship with Preventive Maintenance

2) A few tasks still need to be done in person. This is particularly true with most backup systems. Left in the hands of clients, backups fail.

3) We need to look our clients in the eyes, chat with them, and continually build that relationship

4) It's a great quality control check for ourselves. If you rotate techs and clients each month, the entire team will verify that the entire team is providing excellent service.

If you have clients who are not on managed services, you should still make every attempt to sell a monthly maintenance service. Servers that are maintained live longer. And all servers give off clues to when they are getting ready to fail. But someone has to actually look for those clues. So even today you might be doing a full monthly maintenance "by hand" and not with automated tools.

But you need to do it.

So . . . for the next five chapters, we're simply going to assume that you a monthly maintenance process and that you will make it a central part of your service offering. If you're not convinced yet, I encourage you to dig into these chapters and see how good they are for the quality of service you provide – and for your profitability.

Three Take-Aways from This Chapter:

1. Monthly server maintenance should be a core piece of your service offering.

2. Ideally, each monthly maintenance will have some onsite component, even if most of it is done remotely or done automatically.

3. Start with a long list of items on your MMC – then automate as much as you can.

Three Action Steps for Your Company:

1. _____

   _____

2. _____

   _____

3. _____

   _____

22

Monthly Maintenance Scheduling and Onsite Visits

One of the most important pieces of our business has always been the "monthly maintenance" of client machines. The MMC (monthly maintenance checklist) is primarily used for servers, but you can have an MMC for storage arrays, printers, or anything else you need.

Background: You should run a "Monthly Maintenance" procedure on every contract client every month. If you have a Remote Monitoring and Management (RMM) system, then your list of chores is very short. That's because many things are monitored 24x7 in real time, such as disc space. But you will still need to go to the client's office, shake their hand, look at their server, test the backup, and do some kind of checkup. This is partly tune-up and partly client relations.

For starters, you need a monthly maintenance checklist. That's a list of things you will monitor or do every single month as part of the preventive maintenance that makes managed services work. If you need a place to start, check out my good old 68-point checklist. It's included in the downloadable content included when you register this book.

Once you have your standard checklist, you will refine it for each client. Clients have different backups, different databases, different network setups. So their checklists need to be customized.

You will need to execute four things every month with regard to monthly maintenance jobs:

1) Execute the monthly maintenance checklist at each client

2) Revise all monthly maintenance checklists as needed

3) Make sure the revised MMC is published appropriately and "ready to go" for the next month

4) Each MMC must be filed away for future reference

Obviously, you have a serious time crunch here. No matter whether you have ten clients or a hundred, you need to execute the MMC every month. Someone needs to maintain a calendar so that MMC visits are spaced properly (Clients look puzzled if you show up on the 27th of February and then again on March 1st). This scheduling might be done by the office manager, but is more likely to be done by the tech department. If your PSA (professional services automation) software can create a recurring ticket, then simply have it create one new MMC ticket per client (or per server) each month.

It's a good idea to keep a calendar of when MMCs were executed at each client so you can look back very easily. You almost never need this information, but it's handy when you do.

The revision process is very simple, but needs to be done! If you skip it, you just create more work down the road. Revisions include things like noting that the c:\ drive is too full for logs, so the logs have been moved to the d:\ drive. If that happens, the checklist needs to point to the right place. Normally, revisions are little things like that. Occasionally they are major, such as a new backup procedure.

In a perfect world, the checklist will be updated as the last item on the checklist. But if the tech is onsite, then it will likely wait until he gets back to the office. The problem there is that checklists tend to get thrown on a pile because something more important comes up. If that happens, you need to set aside a date or deadline to get them updated.

As for "publishing," I simply mean that the revised document should be posted on your internal SharePoint site or uploaded to the PSA. We publish these in .pdf format so that they can be accessed and printed off from any computer, including a customer server with no Word program installed.

Finally, you need to file away your MMCs. You might file them all together for one month, or put each one into the appropriate client folder. Which you choose depends on which you think will be more useful down the road. You will need to refer to these when you are looking for problems across clients and when investigating something with a specific client. For technicians, having them all in one place is probably easiest. For billing and client relations, having each client's checklists in the client folder works best. You decide.

All MMCs should be executed by a certain date. They should be updated and published by a certain date. And they should be filed away by a certain date. Every month. No exceptions. Determine who will be responsible for each of these schedules and develop a process.

Documenting the Monthly Maintenance Process

As with all processes, you need to start by defining how your company schedules client maintenance. Then write it out into a procedure. Finally, you need to implement the procedure and train the staff.

To the technicians, all of this simply appears as a series of service requests that need to be scheduled. But to the service manager, these are key client "touch" opportunities. This is particularly true if the client is on a managed service contract. Since most of your patch management and monitoring takes place automatically every day, you might be able to do all of these in a very short period of time for each client. But I recommend that you resist doing it completely remotely.

First, you (meaning you – the service manager) need to have face to face contact with each client from time to time. Never forget that this is a people business. All small businesses are people businesses. And as the face of your business, even casual contact with a client is good.

Second, many backup systems require you to be onsite to verify that they are operating properly. You can look at logs – and even do a restore – remotely. But you can't see whether they're rotating discs (tapes) properly, or tracking jobs in the backup log.

Next, let's look at "major maintenance" and the details of monthly maintenance process. We'll look at what it is exactly, and give you a "real" sample MMC.

Three Take-Aways from This Chapter:

1. Schedule Monthly Maintenance early in the month so that it's always early in the month. Don't put it off.

2. Determine where you will file MMCs when completed – then make sure this policy is followed!

3. If your MMCs have an onsite and a remote component, finish with the remote piece. That leaves the tech at your office – and no excuse for not updating the checklist.

Three Action Steps for Your Company:

1. _____

   _____

2. _____

   _____

3. _____

   _____

23

Checklist for Major Scheduled Maintenance

Most of the time, our maintenance and repair work only affects one desktop, or sometimes a few desktops. But occasionally, we do some work on a server or a piece of equipment that either will or might cause an interruption of critical systems during work hours.

This could be as simple as updating the drivers on a network card. It includes adding rules or features to the firewall, upgrading the line of business application, and making major changes to the Exchange Server or a SQL server used by everyone in the office.

There are two keys to success in this scenario. The first is to take it seriously. I know that sounds obvious, but too many technicians only look at the job (which seems simple) and not at the client (who just wants uptime). The second key to success is communication. You're going to go out of your way to communicate with the client. And if there's a third party technician involved (hardware, software, network, line of business), you will carefully manage all communications with them as well.

Here's our basic Standard Operating Procedure for Major Scheduled Maintenance:

> This document is intended to outline the procedure for implementing scheduled maintenance where any number of services, servers, or networks may experience an interruption that affects more than one person.
>
> 1. It is our preference that all work that may result in service interruption requires one of our technicians to be onsite during the maintenance. That means we will do the work onsite rather than remotely. If work is to be performed by a third-party technician, we would like to be there. We will follow this process whenever practical.
>
> 2. Inform the client technical contact(s) via email as far in advance as possible. Prior notice of one week is ideal. The email must include names of servers, LOBs, and services affected, as well as desired start time and expected duration of interruption.
>
>   A copy of the email should be sent to our support email address with the service ticket number in the subject line. This guarantees that the email parser will attach the email to the appropriate service ticket.
>
> 3. Send an email to client technical contact(s) the day before the scheduled maintenance.
>
> 4. Inform client technical contact(s) via email in the morning of the day of the approved maintenance date.
>
> 5. Inform client technical contact(s) verbally 30 minutes prior to approved maintenance window.
>
> 6. Once the maintenance has been performed, verify that all affected services/servers/LOB applications have been

brought back up and are running properly. Have the client contact verify that everything works.

7. After verifying success, inform client technical contact(s) that the maintenance has been completed.

This process is to be performed by the service manager, or in close association with the service manager. In most cases, the maintenance is routine. But just in case something goes wrong, the service manager needs to know what's going on and must be available to re-route technicians and manage client communications if needed.

Note that the client might be very skittish about any downtime, even if you think it's a ten-second blink. The truth is, stuff can go wrong. That's why we have a policy. Because you have heightened the client's awareness, they might request that the service be moved to another date or time.

The most likely client feedback you'll get is either "That's a good day/time" or "That's a bad day/time." You probably don't know when your clients are performing payroll processing, insurance audits, or other activities that can't give way to simple maintenance. The client will be grateful that you informed them of the procedure and gave them the opportunity to move it to another day.

Checklist for Major Scheduled Maintenance

Client: _____

Project: _____

Service Request/Ticket # _____

_____ Email sent to client informing them of maintenance on
date of: _____

_____ Acknowledgement received for date of: _____

_____ Email sent to client the day before scheduled
maintenance.

_____ Email sent to client on morning of: _____

_____ Client informed 30 minutes prior to maintenance
window.

_____ Maintenance completion date and time: _____

If you have a PSA system, you can create a workflow to make sure these steps are taken. If you don't have a PSA system, you may want to have both the tech and the client rep sign a document on completion of a major project (e.g., a new router installation).

Controlling Firefighters and Heroes

As you know, one of my themes is "Slow Down, Get more Done." This is a case where that's very important. There is a tendency in our business to jump right in, get to work, and start clicking things. But there are times when that's just not the right thing to do.

Most experienced technicians can look back on when they thought everything would go smoothly and it didn't. And the client turned to them and wanted to know what went wrong. Even if the client was very understanding, they still managed to comment that "It would have been nice to have some warning."

This procedure might be overkill most of the time. But on the day that two minutes of expected downtime becomes an hour, you'll be glad you coordinated with the client. This process is normally really uninteresting and just "SOP." But it can go a long way to helping with client relations.

Implementation

Implementing this procedure is simple. Agree to a process similar to that outlined above. Talk to your team and make sure they understand that this is important. (No firefighters needed.)

To the extent you can, build these processes into your PSA system.

This kind of policy requires that everyone on the team

1) Be aware of the policy

2) Practice the policy

3) Correct one another's errors

4) Support one another with reminders

 **Three Take-Aways from This Chapter:**

1. Scheduled maintenance is a perfect time to plan ahead, keep the client informed, and do the job right.

2. This is a good example of over-communicating with the client. The goal is not to "cover your butt" so much as to keep the client informed.

3. If you don't have a folder with email templates, start one. Then create a template for communicating this process.

Three Action Steps for Your Company:

1. _____
   _____

2. _____
   _____

3. _____
   _____

24

The Monthly Maintenance Checklist

Okay. This is it. Let's look at an actual sample of a Monthly Maintenance Checklist. Of course you will customize this for each client. Of course some of your processes and procedures are different. Of course some of this is automated by your RMM (remote monitoring and maintenance) tool. But if you have nothing, this is a great place to start!

As a general practice, we keep all the client monthly maintenance checklists in one folder on the company SharePoint. The main reason for this is that it is much easier to update them all if there's a big change. We could store them in the PSA (professional services automation) tool, but that's only convenient if you are updating checklists one at a time.

Please note, as you read through this, that many of these tasks are much easier if you are onsite. We can do everything remotely. And for a few clients we do that. But for all of our local clients, we go onsite. That way we can make a personal contact. We can talk about issues and point to the notes. We can verify that all those things that say "make sure the client contact does this" are done. And we can see if they've plugged a laser printer into the UPS or piled boxes on top of the server.

Other than section titles, each line begins with a small box suitable for entering a check mark or X. It is critical that everyone understand that the task must be completed before the box is checked.

An editable version of this is included in the downloadable material for this book.

Sample Monthly Maintenance Checklist

Client: Dewey, Cheatum and Howe
            123 4th Street
            Sacramento, CA 95814

Date: _____

Technician: _____

Contact: John Dewey

            916-555-1010

Checklist updated: October 24, 2012

→ Check each box only after the task is complete.

- If an item cannot be done, circle it and write a note to explain.

- If an item does not apply, put an X in the box and write a note to explain.

- If an item needs to be updated, deleted, etc. put edit notes in the left page border and an arrow to the item.

1) Client Check In and Monthly Single*

____ Check with the client contact for any new or outstanding issues and enter them in the "Issues" section of this checklist. (Last page)

____ Check PSA for all outstanding Service Requests that are Not assigned to Back Office.

Print out a prioritized list if necessary.

___ Print out the **Monthly Single** for this month and attach it to this monthly maintenance checklist.

___ Complete all steps detailed in the Monthly Single before continuing on unless specifically noted otherwise in the Monthly Single.

2) Primary Domain Controller/SBS Server Status and Health

___ Make a time stamp entry for the Monthly Maintenance in the Network Documentation Binder Tech Notes.

Note: When performing the Monthly Maintenance remotely, verify the onsite contact has made this entry in the NDB.**

___ Check Windows Event Logs: System, Security, etc. (Record significant errors in Tech Notes)

___ Investigate significant findings from the Event Logs and if necessary add them to the "Issues" section.

___ Print out the Tech Notes file and put it into the Network Documentation Binder.

Note: When performing the Monthly Maintenance remotely, verify the onsite contact has printed, stapled, punched and put the notes into the NDB.

___ (with older Exchange servers) Check incoming and outgoing messages in the Exchange queue to verify there are no spam issues.

___ Check system drive space availability.

C: = _____ Used / _____ Free out of _____ GB

D: = _____ Used / _____ Free out of _____ GB

___ Check system drive fragmentation status.

___ Analysis on C: _____ Setting changes / Problems (if any):

_____

___ Analysis on D: _____ Setting changes / Problems (if any):

_____

___ If any drive is over 1.25 fragmented, schedule a one-time defragmentation of that drive for 5:00 pm.

___ For any system requiring defragmentation, create an SR to check on the status of the defragmentation.

Note: Set the required date of the SR to be the next business days

___ Check UPS logs, UPS run time and if required run any UPS maintenance.

___ Update the Network Documentation Binder Tech Notes with relevant information from this section.

___ Note all unresolved problems from this section in the "Issues" section.

Note: When performing the Monthly Maintenance remotely, verify the onsite contact has made these entries in the NDB.

3) System Backup

___ Check the Backup Job Monitor and Alerts sections, evaluate and clean up as needed.

___ Record the number of good backups in the last 30 days: _____
Note: 20 successful is ideal.

___ Identify the oldest disc(s) or tape(s) in rotation that are indicated to contain a successful backup since the last day of the previous month.

____ Verify that each full server OS backup contained in the target backup set has the complete System State for that server.

____ Verify backup of critical OS files, Data files and Exchange Mailboxes by restoring the following items;

- %System root%\repair directory

- C:\Program Files\Veritas\backup Exec\NT\Catalogs directory

- A sample of files from the clients data directory

Note: All data is redirected to temp\Backup Test

____ Select mailbox items from any active user

Note: All email is redirected to Administrator

____ Log into the Administrator email account and verify the emails targeted for restore were in fact restored.

____ Clean up the Administrator's inbox by moving important company info to the "Keep This" folder in the Inbox and deleting all useless items.

____ Move the media going off site for the End-of-Month Backup to the Retired Media set.

____ If performing the Monthly remotely, perform an Eject Tape function now.

____ Verify that the End-of-Month Tape(s) have been write protected.

____ Record the tapes going off site here: _____

____ Record the number of [tape format and size] Backup Tapes available: _____

____ If there are fewer than 6 tapes available (12 for a two tape scheme, etc.) include this information in the Monthly Maintenance Follow Up Email.

____ Verify the tape drive has been cleaned – Three times for a DAT and once for DLT or SLR.

Note: When performing the Monthly Maintenance remotely have the onsite contact perform the operation and verify they have marked the tape for the number of uses.

____ Cleaning cartridge needed Y / N

____ If a Cleaning Cartridge is needed, include this information in the Monthly Maintenance Follow Up Email.

____ If there is an SR to deliver and label a box of tapes and or a cleaning cartridge, perform the work necessary to complete that SR now.

Note: Be certain to enter the product into the SR immediately.

____ Verify the Backup Log has been updated with notes on:

- - Tape cleaning

- - Restore verification

- - End-of-Month tape(s) going off site

____ Update the Network Documentation Binder Tech Notes with other relevant information from this section.

____ Note all unresolved problems from this section in the "Issues" section.

4) Primary Server Anti-Virus / Anti-Spyware / Spam Filter

____ Verify that the Anti-Virus client on the server is running and scanning on a scheduled basis and that there are no issues to be addressed.

____ Verify that the Server's Anti-Virus client application and definitions are up to date.

____ Verify the Server Anti-Virus client quarantine is empty.

____ Verify that the Network Anti-Virus solution is providing the latest virus definitions.

____ Verify that all Anti-Virus clients are accepting and using the latest virus definitions.

____ Verify that the Anti-Spyware client / solution on the server is running and scanning on a scheduled basis and that there are no issues to be addressed.

____ Verify that any network Spam Filter device is up to date. (firmware or software)

____ Update the Network Documentation Binder Tech Notes with relevant information from this section.

____ Note all unresolved problems from this section in the "Issues" section.

Note: When performing the Monthly Maintenance remotely, verify the onsite contact has made these entries in the NDB.

5) Primary Server System Updates

____ If important patches or updates have been released and approved, apply them to:

- Windows OS

- Exchange Server
- Backup Exec
- Other: _____
- Other: _____

___ Run Microsoft Windows Update repeatedly until all Critical System and Hardware updates are applied.

NOTE: The only hardware updates we do NOT install are Tape Drivers.

NOTE: If rebooting the server is required to continue with the update process or if a NIC driver is being updated, coordinate it with the Client Contact and or users for minimal impact. Use "Golden Hours" for reboots.

Update Notes:

_____

_____

___ Run the latest version of Baseline Security Analyzer. Down load and apply all missing updates indicated.

BSA Notes:

_____

_____

___ Update the Network Documentation Binder Tech Notes with relevant information from this section.

___ Note all unresolved problems from this section in the "Issues" section.

Note: When performing the Monthly Maintenance remotely, verify the onsite contact has made these entries in the NDB.

6) Second Server Status and Health

___ Make a time stamp entry for the Monthly Maintenance in the Network Documentation Binder Tech Notes.

Note: When performing the Monthly Maintenance remotely, verify the onsite contact has made this entry in the NDB.

___ Check Windows Event Logs: System, Security, etc. (Record significant errors in Tech Notes)

___ Investigate significant findings from the Event Logs and if necessary add them to the "Issues" section.

___ Print out the Tech Notes file and put it into the Network Documentation Binder.

Note: When performing the Monthly Maintenance remotely, verify the onsite contact has printed, stapled, punched and put the notes into the NDB.

___ Check system drive space availability.

- C: = _____ Used / _____ Free out of _____ GB
- D: = _____ Used / _____ Free out of _____ GB

___ Check system drive fragmentation status.

___ Analysis on C: _____ Setting changes / Problems (if any):

_____

___ Analysis on D: _____ Setting changes / Problems (if any):

_____

____ If any drive is over 1.25 fragmented, schedule a one-time defragmentation of that drive for 5:00 pm.

____ For any system requiring defragmentation, create an SR to check on the status of the defragmentation.

Note: Set the required date of the SR to be the next business days

____ Check UPS logs, UPS run time and if required run any UPS maintenance.

____ Update the Network Documentation Binder Tech Notes with relevant information from this section.

____ Note all unresolved problems from this section in the "Issues" section.

Note: When performing the Monthly Maintenance remotely, verify the onsite contact has made these entries in the NDB.

7) Second Server System Backup

Note: Server2 does a simple backup to the D drive on Server1. Backup Exec is used to so we can backup the live database.

____ Check the Backup Exec Job Monitor and Alerts sections, evaluate and clean up as needed.

____ Check the job completion time. Verify that Server1 backup starts after Server2 backup finishes.

____ Record the number of good backups in the last 30 days: _____
Note: 20 successful is ideal.

____ Verify that each full server OS backup contained in the target backup set has the complete System State for this server.

____ Verify backup of critical OS files and Data files by restoring the following items;

____ %System root%\repair directory

____ C:\Program Files\Veritas\backup Exec\NT\Catalogs directory

____ A sample of files from the data directory

Note: All data is redirected to temp\Backup Test

____ Verify the Backup Log has been updated with notes on:

- Tape cleaning

- Restore verification

- End-of-Month tape(s) going off site

____ Update the Network Documentation Binder Tech Notes with other relevant information from this section.

____ Note all unresolved problems from this section in the "Issues" section.

8) Second Server Anti-Virus / Anti-Spyware

____ Verify that the Anti-Virus client on the server is running and scanning on a scheduled basis and that there are no issues to be addressed.

____ Verify that the Servers Anti-Virus client application and definitions are up to date.

____ Verify the Server Anti-Virus client quarantine is empty.

____ Verify that the Network Anti-Virus solution is providing the latest virus definitions.

____ Verify that all Anti-Virus clients are accepting and using the latest virus definitions.

___ Verify that the Anti-Spyware client / solution on the server is running and scanning on a scheduled basis and that there are no issues to be addressed.

___ Update the Network Documentation Binder Tech Notes with relevant information from this section.

___ Note all unresolved problems from this section in the "Issues" section.

Note: When performing the Monthly Maintenance remotely, verify the onsite contact has made these entries in the NDB.

9) Second Server System Updates

___ If important patches or updates have been released and approved, apply them to:

- Windows OS

- Backup Exec

- Other: _____

- Other: _____

___ Run Microsoft Windows Update repeatedly until all Critical System and Hardware updates are applied.

NOTE: The only hardware updates we do NOT install are Tape Drivers.

NOTE: If rebooting the server is required to continue with the update process or if a NIC driver is being updated, coordinate it with the Client Contact and or users for minimal impact. Use "Golden Hours" for reboots.

Update Notes:

_____

_____

____ Run the latest version of Baseline Security Analyzer. Down load and apply all missing updates indicated.

BSA Notes:

_____

_____

____ Update the Network Documentation Binder Tech Notes with relevant information from this section.

____ Note all unresolved problems from this section in the "Issues" section.

Note: When performing the Monthly Maintenance remotely, verify the onsite contact has made these entries in the NDB.

10) Other Network, Company and User Specific Items

____ Bandwidth Test via [www.speakeasy.net/speedtest] or

[Other _____]

____ 1st = Download _____ kb/s Upload _____ kb/s

____ 2nd = Download _____ kb/s Upload _____ kb/s

____ (If needed) Cycle the power on the firewall to be sure the maximum number of IP's are free at all times.

____ Update the Network Documentation Binder Tech Notes with relevant information from this section.

____ Note all unresolved problems from this section in the "Issues" section.

Note: When performing the Monthly Maintenance remotely, verify the onsite contact has made these entries in the NDB.

____ Log into the CDP and verify continuous copy of data is functioning correctly and there are no flags or alerts.

____ Purge all old versions of files.

DO NOT DELETE OLD FILES

11) Issues - New and Outstanding (Client Contact, Update section, Users, etc,)

___ _____

___ _____

___ _____

___ _____

___ _____

12) Client Check Out

___ Deliver tape(s) to client contact to be placed offsite.

___ Check with Client Contact and convey status on all outstanding issues.

___ Discuss any recommendations based on this monthly maintenance with the Client Contact.

___ Draft a reminder Email to the Client Contact with the recommendations. Note: You must CC the Service Manager and "Service" mailbox.

____ Make a final round check with all users especially those who had issues to be resolved.

13) Service Requests and Products

____ If required, create Service Requests for all unresolved issues.

____ Update the client's Monthly Maintenance Service request with all of the following;

- Travel Time
- Mileage
- Expenses (e.g., parking)
- Time
- Product delivered to the client. Billable or Not (Tapes, Cleaning cartridges, cables, etc.)
- Detailed work documentation including Internal Analysis notes

→ Monthly Maintenance Complete

14) Monthly Maintenance Checklist Update

____ Update this Monthly Maintenance Checklist document with all necessary revisions.

Notes:

_____

_____

_____

* The "Monthly Single" is a specific task done each month across all clients. We cover this in the next chapter.

** NDB = Network Documentation Binder

After the Monthly Maintenance Checklist

Note that there are two critical items that need attention after the Monthly Maintenance is complete. One is a follow-up email to the client. You can draft this and save it as an .oft file. That way, the tech only makes minor changes, addresses the email, and ends it.

1. Sample Follow-Up Email:

> Hello ,
>
> Your monthly maintenance is complete.
>
> Your server's overall health is excellent.
>
> Backups are working smoothly.
>
> Anti-Virus protection is continuous and the definitions are up to date.
>
> All available system updates have been applied.
>
> As a reminder of what we discussed;
>
> I will follow up on . . .
>
> I created a service request for . . .
>
> We did come across a few things know what point out . . .
>
> There are a few items we need to bring to your attention . . .
>
> Thank you and please contact us if you have any questions.

2. The Issues Section

Finally, you wrote down all the issues you found along the way. These need to be addressed somehow. You need to determine your company procedure for this. You might talk to the client on the spot. Or you might create service requests first and then talk to the client (later?) about any SRs that will result in billable labor. Or the technician onsite might just create SRs and make sure the service manager talks to the client.

Whatever your policy, make sure those issues are followed up.

Final Notes on the Monthly Maintenance Checklist

YES: This is labor intensive. You can save a lot of time with a good RMM tool such as GFI Max, Continuum, or LabTech. But the most important thing – the backup – requires human attention. You can't trust the logs. You can't trust fate. And you can't trust the client to switch hard drives or tapes. You can only trust yourself to verify that this is working.

The labor intensive nature of the MMC is nothing to worry about. On most servers you can do all this in an hour or less. It is time well spent and prevents future problems. It's great for the client relationship, too.

And if nothing else will convince you to go buy an RMM tool, this will. When you have 20 servers that need monthly maintenance, expect to spend 20-25 hours a month executing this. Plus travel time. Now reduce that to 15 minutes each when all you have to check is the backup. Now you're down to 5-6 hours a month. Trust me, a good RMM tool will pay for itself!

Three Take-Aways from This Chapter:

1. Monthly Maintenance cover a LOT of maintenance. That's why it prevents so many problems.

2. You can automate this, but you should price it as if it's always 100% manual. That way, no matter what happens, you'll still make money.

3. Verify that your techs go through this entire process and not just check the boxes. Thus stuff matters!!!

Three Action Steps for Your Company:

1. _____

_____

2. _____

_____

3. _____

_____

25

Monthly Single Checklist

On several occasions I have mentioned a procedure called the "Monthly Single." The Monthly Single evolved as a way for our company to make sure that we maintain a certain level of support across all our clients. In addition to the standard Monthly Maintenance Checklist, we create a single activity that must be completed at every client. Thus "Monthly Single." For a few examples of where this fits, see Volume Two, Chapter Seven on Service Manager Roles and Responsibilities.

The Monthly Single guarantees that we have a certain high level of maintenance across all clients. For example, We verify that all firewalls have the correct ports – and only the correct ports – open across all clients.

Here's the problem and the solution:

The problem this addresses is the general confusion when a company grows. When no one complains, we tend not to give them our time and attention. In the world of break/fix, it's okay to forget about a firewall configuration, time services that will screw up Kerberos authentication, testing backups, passwords for critical accounts, service packs, after-hours emergency call down lists, etc.

But in the world of managed services, you are committing to a higher level of service. So that means you need to be able to assume that ALL of your clients have ALL of their systems tuned up. Everything is under a high level of maintenance. You need to focus on **Preventive Maintenance**. And, to be honest, you have taken on a higher level of responsibility with managed services.

The great fear is this: We have a standard for how servers should be set up. But we manage lots of servers. If we set them up from scratch, we're good to go. But we inherit a lot of servers, firewalls, printer, etc. And even when we adopt a standard policy across all clients, we have to go verify that it's implemented across all the existing clients.

The Monthly Single Process

Each month, you choose one specific task that will be executed at each client. One of the items in the Monthly Maintenance Checklist is to "Complete the Monthly Single."

You should track this via a separate service ticket in your PSA for each client. When that's closed, the Monthly Single is completed.

It is a good idea to create a separate folder for all your Monthly Single procedures so you have them all in one place. This also makes it easy for you to repeat a procedure. For example, if you scan all the client's printed documentation to PDF once a year, you can start with the procedure you used last year.

This folder might contain an Excel Spreadsheet that lists which procedure was used per month. We find it is very handy to name the files with the date information and the task to be completed. For example:

- Monthly Single - 201410 - Time Services.docx

- Monthly Single - 201411 - Service Packs.docx

- Monthly Single - 201412 - Change Master Password.docx

- Monthly Single - 201501 - EOY Documentation.docx

In this way, you can see at a glance what was done and when.

Examples

Here are some ideas for Monthly Single tasks you might implement:

- Verify that each client's router, firewall, and domain registration information is in the PSA

- Verify that [your preferred spyware tool] is installed on every desktop

- Make sure Veritas Backup Exec is using family naming for tapes, with Job, Date, and Time in the family name

- Verify that time services are enabled on all servers and configured correctly throughout the organization

- Train primary client contacts to use the Client Service Portal

- Verify internal and external DNS settings

- Photocopy all client's physical documentation to PDF

- Verify that a recent critical fix has been applied to all servers/workstations as needed

- Verify and record server build dates

- Verify Router setup and firewall setup in PSA

- Verify that only correct devices are plugged into UPSs

- Update client call-down lists for emergencies
- Review hidden updates in Microsoft update and apply as needed
- Evaluate backup scheme and implement changes if needed
- Perform complete UPS stress test to determine actual uptime
- Photograph server room and equipment racks - put in PSA
- Verify network map in Network Documentation Binder. Fix as needed.
- Verify that our preferred group policies have been implemented

It is always a good idea to keep an eye out for future Monthly Singles. For example, if a specific software change is released, the Monthly Single is a good way to roll it out in an orderly fashion and verify that it was completed for every client.

Three Take-Aways from This Chapter:

1. Create your own list of important tasks that need to be done once per year at each client.

2. Implement this new process with training. It's different and will take some shepherding to complete the first month.

3. Verify that all customized Monthly Maintenance Checklists include a checkbox for the Monthly Single.

Three Action Steps for Your Company:

1. _____

   _____

2. _____

   _____

3. _____

   _____

26

Outsourcing (Some) Of Your Monthly Maintenance

In the last few chapters we've covered *Why We Do Monthly Maintenance, Monthly Maintenance Scheduling and Onsite Visits, The Monthly Maintenance Checklist*, and the *Monthly Single Checklist*. All of that is about how YOU manage monthly maintenance. In other words, it lists all the various chores and checks you need to do each month.

But there are three tiers of checklist activities: Automatic, manual remote, and manual onsite. Let's look at each of these briefly.

1) Monitored automatically. These items can be removed from monthly maintenance once it is clear that we'll never miss a critical alert.

In a modern managed service business, you will be using some kind of remote monitoring and management tool (RMM). So many items on the checklist are checked every minute of every day instead of once a month. This includes "stop sign" error messages, whether critical services are running, free disc space, and all the other things that can be monitored automatically.

It is still important to occasionally have a human being review the server logs. Some errors will show up as patterns there but never reach a point where they will trigger an alert or service ticket.

Sidebar: Knowing "Normal" When You See It

One of the most important skills for troubleshooting is experience. See the discussion of troubleshooting skills in Volume Three, Chapter Twenty-Nine.

But how do you give technicians experience except to simply have them show up for work year after year? How do you build the "muscles of success" that allow them to get a sense when something's not quite right?

You understand "normal" only by seeing what's normal hundreds of times, or thousands of times. For example, we have technicians actually open the server logs and read through them so that they know what to look for. Almost every system has "normal" errors that can be ignored.

A great example of this is the error that shows up every day when an Exchange server cannot synch with another Exchange server. Well, if you only have one, then it's okay to ignore that error. But you need to know that.

When an emergency happens, one of the most important troubleshooting tools you have is the event log. But if you never look at it, then you don't know what "normal" is. As a result, you will get distracted by yellow and red errors that are scary but perfectly normal. You just don't know what normal is.

Here's another example: Backups. Notice in the Monthly Maintenance Checklist that twenty or more successful backups is considered "good." Here's why: In the average month, the disc (or tape) won't get changed once. The backup job won't finish for some reason once. The backup job will be stopped once. Stuff happens. But you are only comfortable with that stuff if you see it all the time and know that that's the way life is.

What's a normal operating temperature for a server? Well, that varies from server to server. But if you look at the temperature for the first time ever during an emergency, you won't have any idea what that number means. Is it high or low? I don't know. You don't know.

The power of knowing "normal" is that you can return to normal. You can return a system to normal once you know what it is. We all have some vague idea about normal from simply working with computers. But the very specific normal that applies to a specific server is only knowable when you see it all the time.

. . . And that's why we keep a human element in the process, even when we can automatically monitor a lot of stuff. It trains us on normal and makes us familiar with the tools for managing the servers.

2) Some checklists can be completed remotely. These items can be completed by you or by your outsourced helpdesk. It makes sense to outsource these tasks because remote is remote, as long as the monitoring is done correctly. So why would we do it ourselves?

Examples:

- Check defragmentation level and, if over 1.25, schedule a forced defrag

- Check for yellow "Warning Signs" in the system logs. These often do not trigger an alert, but if you have 100/day then you probably have a problem.

- Perform internet speed tests

3) Some checklists require you to go onsite. These items require a technician onsite. So we go.

Examples:

- UPS tests (unplug the UPS and verify how long it goes before losing power. You need to plug is back in.

- Verify backup, label media (disc or tape) for offsite storage, and give them to the appropriate person

- Update the Network Documentation Binder Tech Notes with relevant information

The Bottom Line

We have basically turned over 99% of our monthly maintenance to our RMM provider/outsourced helpdesk. Their agent handles the automated piece and their NOC handles the remote piece. The thing we just haven't been able to hand off completely has been complete maintenance of the backup systems. Some things have to be done in person and clients are amazingly unwilling to take this seriously.

So backups fall into the category of "We are taking care you because you refuse to take care of yourself." Counting the number tapes on the shelf cannot be handled by a remote technician. Maybe we'll install web cams for this.

The key to working with any outsourced helpdesk – whether they are in your country or somewhere else – is *precise communication*. I've heard so many people explain that outsourced helpdesk personnel don't know how to do things, don't do it right, and don't communicate well.

Here's the deal: You need to **delegate, not abdicate**. You need to provide excellent instructions that are extremely carefully worded. You need to take control of the communication process and make sure that they understood what you said. You need to check back frequently and verify their work.

In other words, you need to give them as much attention as you would give any other employee.

If I said to you, "Configure this firewall," there is almost no chance that you would do so to my satisfaction. I need to give you detailed instructions of what I want – and a checklist. Then you will be perfectly successful. Your outsourced helpdesk is the same way.

Consider this: If YOU can do it remotely, or a really good technician could do it remotely, then turn it over to your outsourced helpdesk. Let them do it remotely. And the better you are at managing them, the better they'll respond.

Three Take-Aways from This Chapter:

1. It is important that you understand what your automated RMM tools can do. Use them to the extent of their abilities!

2. Prepare carefully for turning over work to your outsourced helpdesk. After the first job, evaluate what happened and fine-tune the process. Ask them for their feedback.

3. Learn normal. Create "normal" inside your business and with your clients' computers. Everyone in your company should know your normal.

Three Action Steps for Your Company:

1. _____

    _____

2. _____

    _____

3. _____

    _____

Section III –

Service Focus: Backups and Disaster Recovery

27

Designing a Great Backup Process

In the last section I told you how Monthly Maintenance was one of the pillars on which I built my managed service business. Another is backups. I am passionate about backups. I'm obsessive about backups. A huge piece of my business is based on the fact that we place backups above everything else.

As you may recall from Chapter Seven, tickets move to higher priority status when backups fail. One might be within normal operating parameters. Two failures in a row is a problem. Three failures in a row is an urgent matter that needs your attention.

Here are some things I believe:

- Most backup systems don't work.

- Most companies don't have a good backup system.

- The easier it gets to provide a good backup, the less likely it is that companies have a good backup.

I am absolutely convinced that testing backups is the highest priority task for a managed service provider. Clients may not think that – until the day the fire truck is pulling away from their building.

That's why the last seven chapters in this four-book set are dedicated to backups. The worst thing that can happen to your client's business is the loss of all data. You've seen it happen. You know it can happen. Preparing to survive a disaster is the greatest service you can provide.

Warning:

In the next few chapters, I'm going to say some things that most technicians don't want to hear. I try not to be arrogant, but someone has to say this. And it's better to say it here – deep inside a set of books that your clients will never read – than on the front page of a magazine.

Why Backups Fail

Here's an alarming statistic for you: When we take on a new client, there's a 50% chance that they don't have a working backup. They often THINK they have a working backup, but they don't. This number is alarmingly consistent after twenty years. It might even be increasing.

The most common scenario is that the client paid someone to set up their backup system. That person created a "set it and forget it" strategy and walked away. Now, perhaps years later, the company has no idea that they don't have a backup at all.

There are three primary reasons that backups don't work:

1. The person who set up the backup did not understand the hardware or software.

2. "Something" stopped working and never got restarted or fixed.

3. Improper management of the media (tape, disc, images, etc.).

Now, you might have heard a hundred excuses for why backups fail. But, in the end, it is always one of these three things. So while there might be an unlimited number of variations on a theme, there are only really three key things you need to have for success.

As simple as it sounds, you need:

1. Competent installation and setup of the backup system.

2. Proper maintenance as time goes on.

3. A working plan for managing the media.

One of my frustrations has always been the "bad" reputation tape backup has in the small business environment. I believe tape has this bad reputation because it used to require complicated knowledge (SCSI), because technicians don't want to design a working backup strategy, and because clients don't bother to change tapes.

The lessons: You can build a horrible backup based on perfectly reliable technology. Your backup is only as good as its execution. And clients don't care about their backup until it's time for disaster recovery.

It is a simple fact that tape is the most successful medium ever invented for backup and disaster recovery. Let me share 1,000 data points to support this: Every single one of the Fortune 1,000 uses tape backup. It is the ultimate backup solution for several reasons.

First, tape is portable. That makes the offsite part much easier.

Second, tape lasts. You can read a magnetic tape that's 20 or 30 years old with no problems – if you bought the right tape in the first place.

Third, tape is reasonably priced. I know it hurts to take a $79 tape offsite "forever." But that compares very favorably to a hard disc at $99.

Fourth, tape allows us to easily access multiple points of backup. That means multiple versions of files and multiple opportunities to restore.

Anyway, you don't have to use tape. But it's absurd to say that tape sucks or that tape backups fail. Tape is critical to the likes of Google and Amazon. But they are willing to spend time and effort to use it properly. For reasons why you might use something else, see Chapter Thirty-Two.

Why Do We Do Backups?

Let's step back a minute and look at why we do backups. In a true, major disaster, you may not be able to get to your office. Consider recent floods in the Midwest, hurricane Katrina, the five-day electrical outages from a few years ago, and Super Storm Sandy. It is quite realistic that you could be kicked out of your office and need to relocate. Yes, the chances are slim, but it's your job to take responsibility for the client's business.

On more of a day-to-day basis, "stuff" happens. Someone deletes an important file. The database becomes corrupt. You discover on Thursday that you saved the wrong version of a spreadsheet last Monday. Sometimes we can restore from the local Volume Shadow Copy. You might have a local backup archive. It is vitally important that you have multiple point-in-time backups.

Backups become a legal point-in-time snapshot. Backups become a financial point-in-time snapshot. More and more small businesses are finding that they're being held responsible for archiving email and other important data. Sometimes these requirements come from the State Legislature, sometimes from the courts.

The All-Important Media

So you've decided to back up your data. The next topic is: what media should you use? Most people are tempted to use whatever's handy, easy, cheap, and readily available. Those are all horrible criteria.

When will you need your backup? Five years from now. During a flood. During a fire. When you can't get to your office. When you're stressed out in the middle of an emergency and you need your business back in business right away!

Chapter Thirty-Two examines the various technology options and how you can make good choices. Just remember that there are many bad choices for backups. "Bad" generally means some media that will be useless when you really need it. The most common example is a format for which you cannot find a reader. Zip Disks are a great example of this. How many businesses have boxes full of useless Zip Disks, and no way to read the data?

When people tell me they're "backing up" to USB drives, I shudder. First, they may not be backing up at all. One of the worst disaster recoveries I have ever been involved in was an ISP that did backups to USB drive. Drag. Drop. Done. He did this for a year. He explained to me that it was blazingly fast.

When disaster struck (employee vandalism), we went to use the backup. Every file was 1KB. He had a USB drive with hundreds of thousands of shortcuts to the original files. His backup had absolutely nothing on it! (We did eventually save his data, but not from his "backup system." It was very, very expensive.)

We'll talk more about this later, but most USB backups give you one copy of your data. If you configure them right, you might get two or three copies. Then you're done. No end of month. No media rotation to improve chances for recovery. No offsite.

Tape might be a bad backup medium for you if you are not willing to learn how to set up the hardware, configure the software, and design a strategy that covers all of your requirements for restore points (see the next two chapters).

The Average Disaster Recovery

The primary technicians in our company have been working with computers since before the "personal computer" was invented. We've seen disasters. And we've recovered many a company from disaster. Generally speaking, here's how a disaster recovery flows in the real world:

1. For whatever reason, the first backup option (medium) isn't available. Perhaps the failure came in the middle of the backup job. Perhaps the server with the backup tape was destroyed. Perhaps the tape was bad. Perhaps the user didn't change tapes that day.

2. The second backup option is good and almost complete. As with all things in life, it's the "almost" that costs the most money. Almost might mean everything except five files. Or everything except yesterday's data.

In most cases, we can go get that other 5% or 1% that's missing. But you have to decide how much you want to pay for that last little bit. You've heard of the 80/20 rule. Well, in disaster recovery, there's the 95/5 and the 99/1 rules. Recovering the last five percent of the data will be 95% of the total recovery cost. Recovering the last one percent will take 99% of the total cost of data recovery.

Here's why USB backups are troublesome:

- Perception of safety. Backup to hard drive is easy to understand. That doesn't make it good.

- Too few points of failure. We really like the belt-and-suspenders approach. In a perfect world, we will have VSS, onsite images, onsite tapes, offsite tapes, and five other ways to recover your data. If you have a single USB drive, you have one device. If it fails, you're done. No backup. No recovery. Just disaster. If you have two USB drives, and you go back and forth between them, you have two points of recovery. If one is onsite during the disaster, you're back to one.

- Limited number of backups. Let's say you have 50GB of data, and you have two 300GB drives. That gives you six copies of your data on each drive.

  Monday - Tuesday - Wednesday - Thursday - Friday - Monday

  plus

  Tuesday - Wednesday - Thursday - Friday - Monday - Tuesday

  No end of month. No end of quarter. No end of year. No archive. No legal snapshot. No financial snapshot.

Let's say the office above yours has a water leak and your server spends the weekend with water dripping all over it. Poof. Gone. Now you have lost one backup disc and six opportunities for recovery. The newest backup is now seven days old.

Remember the lessons of history. The first available backup option isn't good for some reason. Now you have five points of backup and the newest is eight days old. On that day, the Exchange server backup was not complete. So some people have lost all email for nine days.

You get the point, I hope.

We like to design systems that provide multiple points of backup – onsite and offsite – to maximize recoverable data and minimize the time it takes for recovery.

Security Note

Please don't forget the obvious security concern. If you really do what you say you're going to do, you need to take your backup off site.

Over the years, we've had clients have their backups stolen. Not necessarily on purpose. They leave the backup in their car, or their purse, or their brief case, or their computer bag. etc. If a thief finds himself with your backup tape, chances are very good he'll throw it away.

If he finds a USB drive, he's very likely to plug it into a computer and see what's there. What's there? Six opportunities to steal all the information in your company.

Internet Backups

Of course cloud-based backups have become much more common, and reliable, in the last decade. Most of the commercial-quality services are pretty good. But they all tend to have one of four basic problems:

- The cost is high, no matter how cheap it seems in the sales literature.

- In order to make the system work, clients with a small budget only back up a tiny fraction of their data.

- Most people have very slow outbound internet connections. So, getting a good image of their data will take too long. You solve this by shipping a hard drive with all or their company data across the country.

- Fast recovery in case of a disaster is dependent on the client's download speed. See item #3.

The cost of Internet backups is still high. We are now commonly looking at terabytes of data – at about one dollar per GB per month. Where a client used to have 50GB of storage and pay $500/month, they now have 500 GB of storage . . . and pay $500/month. The price has really gone down!

In order to make the system affordable, some people only back up a tiny fraction of your data. When you ask vendors about costs, or mention how expensive it is, here's their answer: "Most companies choose to only backup their most vital data in this method."

Whoa. In our mind, such a service has very limited purpose. One of the most important purposes of a backup is disaster recovery. So if you only back up, say, ten of the five hundred gigabytes of data, how do you get the other information back?

If your building burns down, floods, or is unavailable because of Hazardous Waste spill, how do you recover your systems and get back in business? Really. Think about this. What use is there to such a "backup?"

In our perfect world, we will install temporary equipment (or replacement equipment) as quickly as possible. Then we'll configure the hardware and reload an image of the operating system and software. Once everything's up, we'll restore the most recent version of the data. This should all be done within the first business day.

With a combination of onsite backups (disc-to-disc, BDR, etc.) and off site backup (disc or tape), we can do this in less than a day.

BDR – Backup and Disaster Recovery

BDR devices emerged about ten years ago and have some amazing features that solve many challenges with backup and disaster recovery.

Basically, a BDR is intended to provide near-real-time backup or imaging of a machine. Some work by actually creating a "live" standby image of a server, with replication every few minutes. Some can spin up the live standby machine into a temporary version of your sever when the server fails. Almost all of them allow further backup by copying the BDR backup or image to an offsite server. The offsite version may be in a cloud service or at your own data center, depending on the product.

BDRs generally allow granular file restore as well as whole image restores. Some maintain a large number of file versions as well. All of them are intended to provide a very quick "disaster recovery" – meaning that you can get some version of your server back and in business when the server fails. Some do this with quick restores, some by spinning up a virtual version of your server on the BDR device, and others by spinning up an image of your server in a cloud environment.

It is *extremely* important that you understand this technology if you use it. You must still master a knowledge of how many actual restore points you have, how you would recover under various circumstances, and how you're going to test the backup to verify that it's doing what you think it's doing.

BDR devices really with backup to the cloud really demonstrated their value during the electrical outages caused by "Superstorm Sandy" in 2012. Those that were set up properly and tested regularly saved their owners millions of dollars.

Disc and Tape Procedures

Let's flesh out some specifics on using hard drives and tapes for backup. We want our backup to provide fast recovery in a disaster, permanent long-term storage, and easy access for the occasional lost or corrupted file.

Consistent procedures save us money, stop us from making mistakes, and support our ability to send any tech into any client. There are only a handful of things you need to know about these backups.

Here's what we do NOT do:

We do not perform "grandfather-father-son" backups. That would mean never being able to go back more than two versions, and using the same discs or tapes dozens, or hundreds, of times.

We do not do "M-T-W-Th-F" backups. Again, there's not much rotation here and the same discs or tapes are used forever.

Here is our preferred Backup Procedure

Discs/tapes are numbered sequentially. For example, 101, 102, 103, 104, 105 or 1001, 1002, 1003, 1004, 1005. When you move to a different form factor, the sequence is changed (e.g., from 101 . . . to 1001 . . .).

Discs/tapes are used sequentially. For example, 101, 102, 103, 104, 105 or 1001, 1002, 1003, 1004, 1005. Obviously, if a disc/tape is not available, that number is skipped and the next available number is used.

We do a full backup every night. If this is not possible, we will develop an alternative, inform the client, and try to move to a system that can achieve a full backup.

Ideally, the backup is taken off site every night. A courier service from the storage company will pick up the tape(s). Some companies only do this once a week.

Make sure the person who does this does not put discs/tapes in a purse or briefcase and then never take them home. And you must never bring a tape "back" until another disc/tape has gone home.

We log all backups in a paper log. The log should contain the disc/tape number, job name, and the date the disc/tape is placed in the drive. In a perfect world, someone will look at the backup log each morning to determine whether the backup is successful. This might be the client or one of your technicians.

We like to keep 7-10 discs/tapes in rotation. With a five-day backup, this gives us more than a full week of backups (assuming that some tapes are off site).

At least once a month, we test a select tape or disc from the backup to verify that we have a good backup, and we can restore from it. This will be our monthly off site tape or disc.

This monthly off site should be the smallest-numbered recent disc/tape.

This monthly off site is not intended to ever come back!

That last point is critical. When your monthly off site discs/tapes go off site, they have no return day. We do not use discs/tapes again and again until they are unreliable. Yes, it costs money. Consider it cheap insurance. The less a medium is used, the more reliable it is.

These are also your legal and financial snapshots.

With this system, we can restore data from any business day in the last ten to fourteen days. If we absolutely have to, we can go to the previous monthly off site media. Or the month before that, etc.

Remember that one of our goals was to have as many recovery points as possible. This system gives us 7-10 recovery points for the last two weeks, plus an additional 12 recovery points for the previous year.

With a system like that, it would be very difficult to NOT be able to get your company back in business. When you add on site systems such as BDR, data mirroring, and disc-to-disc backup, then you're even safer.

Where do things go wrong?

Perhaps the biggest mistake that's made by technicians and business owners is to Set It And Forget It.

It is very common to set up a backup system so that the only thing the client needs to do is to switch the disc or tape every day. The cartridge pops out. They switch it. End of loop. Repeat forever.

There are three major problems with this. First, this process does not include any ongoing test of the backup. 99% of the time, the backup worked fine when the original technician walked out the door. But it could have stopped working the next day. So, a year later, when you need to restore something, there's nothing there.

Second, the most common scenario (which we never do) is to create a very small rotation, such as grandfather-father-son. You've got three sets of media. You write over the same three again and again and again until the magnetic media turns to dust. You couldn't get data off these media if your life depended on it.

Third, stuff happens. Tape drives and hard drives eventually break. A job might only be set to restart after a successful finish. So, once a job fails to finish, it will never run again. Updates to the operating system can cause backups to fail. You might move your data to a new location. Or you might add a database that's not on the backup. Or expand your systems. Over time, you're not backing up everything.

In some cases, your data has grown and you now need two media for each backup. That means that you're switching out cartridges and finishing Monday's backup at 9:00 AM on Tuesday. No second cartridge on Tuesday means that the Tuesday backup doesn't start until you switch cartridges on Wednesday, etc. Or the Monday backup doesn't finish and the backup job is not re-started.

Backups are vitally important to your clients. They're like insurance. You don't need it until you need it. Then you really need it!

How do you fix all this? Simple maintenance.

The "fix" for all these problems is very easy. Someone needs to occasionally open up the log files and:

- Make sure the backup is properly configured (backing up everything you need, not skipping vital info)
- Make sure the backups are running

- Make sure the backups are completing

- Determine whether the backup still fits on one tape or media set

- Reconfigure as needed

Add a monthly test restore to the process and it will take about half an hour per month.

This final point brings us back to tape management. One of the key elements of a successful recovery is having good media. It is no surprise, then, that one of the key failure points for backup systems is related to media. This is another area where proper care is not difficult, you just have to do it. Proper media management means:

1. You have a large rotation. Recall the earlier discussion of rotations and recovery points. If you have a Grandfather-Father-Son rotation and your backup goes to two media, you can't even have one complete "extra" backup. So if one cartridge is bad, you may never have a single complete backup.

   With a rotation of 10-15 discs or tapes, no single media is used too many times. And if you use the lowest-numbered media at the end of the month, and take them offsite for the permanent offsite storage, then no media will ever be over-used. This simple procedure has a dramatic effect on successful recovery.

   In the mid-1990's I was the Site Manager for PC Software Support at HP's Roseville plant. We managed about 5,000 desktops with about 7,000 computers overall. Oddly enough, part of my job included managing the person who switched the backup tapes. Yes, that was a fulltime job. You see, HP does a 365 day rotation. That means that each tape is only used once per year. Now, there are thousands of tapes in the system. So, if you want a hint about how seriously big companies take tape management, that's it. Your system will be less complicated.

2. Backup media are stored properly. Do not store discs or tapes in your purse or briefcase where they can be stolen. Do not store them in your car where they can freeze or get too hot. Do not store them in a plastic bag.

True Story

We had a client who sent all the backup tapes home with an employee. One day they needed to recover a file that had been deleted many months before. We instructed the employee to bring in the backup tapes.

No Kidding: They were in a plastic bag that had been stored in the freezer. Someone told her to store important papers there. Tapes are more important that papers, right?

There was frost in the bag, which turned to water. While most of the water was gone, it took a long time to dry out the tapes.

Note, please, that we did recover the data! That's the beautiful thing about tape. If you're dedicated to success, tape will come through every time. We probably would not have had this kind of luck with a USB drive.

But, please, do not tempt fate by storing your tapes in the freezer.

Three Take-Aways from This Chapter:

1. Most backups fail due to improper setup, improper maintenance, or improper management of the media.

2. Before you define a backup, determine which kind of restore jobs you want to provide for. Which restore points do you need?

3. You don't have to use a complicated system, but don't assume that a simple system will work just because it's easy to set up.

Three Action Steps for Your Company:

1. _____

   _____

2. _____

   _____

3. _____

   _____

28

Defining Your Client Backup

Sometimes you have to cut through all the hundreds of things you do for clients and get to the absolute basics. The most time consuming "basic thing" we do is to maintain computers and networks. That maintenance is probably the second most important thing we do. The most important thing we do is to prepare for something that almost never happens: Building and testing backups.

Clients rarely understand the importance of backups. If they did, the number of new clients with working backups would be much higher. Until a client has experienced a truly catastrophic data loss, they just don't put much emphasis on backups. And of course backups are completely useless without a good restore from backup!

As with most modern technology, backups have what I call the **Paradox of Simplicity**: It's easy ENOUGH that anyone can create a bad backup system that appears to be good enough. When a client (or an incompetent technician) creates a half-baked, "good enough" network, it will be a slow network that has more equipment failures than a professional network. Maybe that's good enough.

But a "good enough" backup is not good enough. If you can't recover data, or can't recover all data, the client is likely to go out of business! If you need scary stats on this, read the excellent report by HP and SCORE entitled "Impact on U.S. Small Business of Natural & Man-Made Disasters." See www.webwizebackup.com/impactofDisaster.pdf

This is a great report to hand out to clients as it does not push any solutions, but merely raises awareness of the potential consequences of data loss.

We have always made backups an extremely important part of the service we offer. Failed backups are the task guaranteed to raise the assigned priority of a service request. And testing backups are part of every monthly maintenance for every client. Taking backups offsite is a monthly task.

So let's dig in.

Defining Your Client Backup

There was a time when a backup was very simple to define: Backup everything every day. That might have been a challenge when you were using 8 GB tapes and wondering whether you were going to have to go to a larger-capacity tape drive.

Now we have gargantuan databases and monster hard drives that seem to just show up. It's not unusual for clients to have multiple terabyte drives. And we all know that data expands to fill the space available. Whether it's log files, streaming media files, on-the-fly backups, vacation photos, or serious business data. It gets bigger and more diverse every year.

Inventory the Data

As you can see, you need to define the data your client has. In a perfect world, nothing important is kept on the desktop. But you need to find out for sure. After that you can turn to the server(s) and catalog all the resources that need to be backed up. Databases, directories, system state, etc. List out everything that's on the server and the format it's in (SQL, EDB, flat file, etc.).

Consolidate the Data

I know this is easier said than done. Basically, you need to get that data off the desktops, stray USB drives, etc. and onto the server where you can back it all up as part of the backup job.

Define the Backup Job(s)

Defining a backup means exactly that: What will you backup? When will you back it up? Onto what medium will you back it up? For example, let's look at three fictional clients.

1. Client: Able Baker Charlie

      Backup: Full backup of server "Obiwan"

      When: Every workday (M-F) at 11:00 PM

      Medium: DAT 160 tape with Symantec Backup Exec Software

2. Client: Cousin Larry's Pretty Good Accounting

      Backup One: "Public" data on server SBS2011

      When: Mon-Wed-Fri at 11:00 PM

Medium: Disc-to-Disc to SAN - then SAN to cloud

Backup Two: System and user data on server SBS2011

When: Every Friday at 11:00 PM

Medium: Disc-to-Disc to SAN - then SAN to cloud

3. Client: KPEnterprises

Backup One: Full backup of server "Tommy"

When: Every workday (M-F) at 9:00 PM

Medium: Disc-to-Disc to Server Elvis

Backup Two: Full image backup of server "Tommy"

When: Every Saturday at 10:00 PM

Medium: Acronis

Backup Three: Full backup of server "Elvis"

When: Every workday (M-F) at 10:00 PM

Medium: DAT 160 tape with Symantec Backup Exec Software

Backup Four: Full image backup of server "Elvis"

When: Every Saturday at 11:30 PM

Medium: Acronis

Why don't we simply backup everything every night for every client? Well, some clients don't need it. But more likely than that, you may be working with two limited resources: Time and capacity. Depending on the hardware and network involved, you may not be able to move all of the data to the backup device in a reasonable amount of time. Or the medium (whether disc or tape) may not be large enough to hold all of the data.

In either case, you have to decide what to backup and when. The system state probably doesn't change much. Line of business databases, Exchange, and core data files change every day. You have to calculate what goes where, how long each job will take, and how much will fit on a given medium.

If you have a BDR solution, you should be backing up everything every day. Maybe even every fifteen minutes.

Why Document This Way?

There are many reasons to document what you do. They pretty much all apply here. You need to be able to assure the client that everything is being backed up, and that it's on a schedule consistent with their restore requirements in case of a disaster. You need to be able to send various technicians to the job site and know that they will be able to figure it out when they need to restore a file. And if you get hit by a bus, this stuff needs to be written down so it can be carried out while you're recovering in the hospital.

One of my rules for life is Slow Down, Get More Done. Restoring a server from backup is a perfect example of that. Think about how you will restore a server. The first medium you'll need is the O.S. and system state. Ideally, that will have everything you need to boot onto that server and finish the restore. So what's the next medium you need? And the next? If you have separate media for the system state and data, which is the most recent of each?

Think slowly. If you get this wrong, you'll double the time for your restore, or worse.

How exactly will you restore this server?

Once you can precisely define the restore process, then you'll be able to verify that you have a good backup process, and that it's properly documented. Now take yourself out of the picture. Can a qualified technician look at your process and properly restore this server? If the answer is "no" or "I don't know" then you need to keep working on it.

Implementation Notes

As we'll see in the next chapter, your backup documentation is primarily a narrative. It's easy, but technically precise. If you get it wrong, you'll end up over-writing a backup you need. If that happens, the restore will be troublesome.

Precision matters - a lot.

Be A Little Bit Afraid

This is a true story. On more than one occasion, we have had to deal with a client who went to restore files from their backup tape and screwed up their backup. The most common problem is this:

The backup is waiting for a new medium (tape or disc). The client removes the old and puts in the disc or tape from which they need to restore files.

The running backup has been waiting for a new medium, sees it, formats it, and proceeds to complete the backup. The client sees blinking lights and thinks everything's okay – until he opens the backup program and sees that it's backing up to the critical medium he just fed it.

The main thing you need to do is to educate your team about your company's approach to backups (and restores), and then make sure everyone who might be involved in a restore has an opportunity to put their hands on a backup. They need to be comfortable with this so they can be successful after a disaster.

They need to know "normal" so that there is zero panic during an emergency. A restore is a restore. Go slow. Be successful.

You may have only one or two people on your team that would ever be involved in an emergency restore. But every technician should be involved with monthly tests and setting up backup jobs. That ensures a high level of knowledge across your team. This is literally *insurance* for you. If one of your technicians ever needs to make a decision about a medium to use, you want to do everything you can to make sure they make good decisions.

This kind of policy requires that everyone on the team

1) Be aware of the process

2) Practice the process

3) Correct one another's errors

4) Support one another with reminders

Three Take-Aways from This Chapter:

1. Go slow and be more successful.

2. Everyone on your team should know and understand backups as thoroughly as possible.

3. One day, consider reviewing the definitions you have for each client's backups. Are they right? Is this what's actually been scheduled? Make changes as needed.

Three Action Steps for Your Company:

1. _____

   _____

2. _____

   _____

3. _____

   _____

29

Documenting Backups

As I've pointed out in *The Network Documentation Workbook* and in many presentations, there two weaknesses at virtually every new client we take on. The first is documentation and the second is backup.

Approximately 99% of the new clients we've brought on board since 1995 have had little or no documentation of their computer systems. The documentation is at the consultant's house, in his head, or nowhere at all. Sometimes there's a crappy little folder with a printout from the ISP and a couple of piece of paper with chicken scratching. But that's it.

As for backups, our experience has been amazingly consistent. As I mentioned in the last chapter, almost exactly 50% of all new clients have no working backup when they come to us. They might think they have a backup, but it's not working. It's never tested. No one knows when it stopped working. Whatever the case may be, they don't have a working backup.

This chapter is about overcoming these two weaknesses where it matters most: how you document your backup.

Overview

First, you need a backup. In the big picture, our backups follow some variation on the following elements:

- Data are stored on the server

- Data are backed up locally

- The backup is moved offsite

Each of those has some caveats. When clients don't or won't store data on the server, we might institute a Robocopy job to copy data to the server every night. Backup might be disc or tape locally, or even my favorite: "disc-disc to tape" (DDT) or disc-disc to cloud (DDC). Eventually, we want all data to be moved off site.

It is critically important that you document your backup. I know it seems simplistic, but you really might get hit by a bus and not come in one day.

Documentation takes two forms. At a minimum, you should have a *narrative*. That means, one simple paragraph for each step of the process. You might also create a diagram. The tools and procedures need to be spelled out so that another competent computer consultant can follow your instructions.

Notice that I did NOT say that the client needs to be able to follow these instructions. Some clients will, some won't. But when you get hit by a bus and the client brings in another competent computer consultant to save their business, that person will understand what you write.

Here's a sample backup description:

Backup Description

All data is stored on the server in the x:\data directory. No data are stored on the desktops. The only exceptions to this are that the QuickBooks files, financial reports, and personnel records are in the x:\moola directory.

Users "My Documents" folders are not redirected to the server.

Once a week the Backup job "Weekly Full" runs on the server and backs up everything to disc on the NAS-1000 storage device. This includes the server O.S., Exchange, etc. Everything. This job is scheduled for 8:00 PM on Friday night. It is normally finished by midnight.

Every night the Backup job "Daily" runs on the server and backs up the Exchange databases and the data drive (This is physical drive "D" on the server). This backup goes to disc on the NAS-1000 storage device. This job is scheduled for 10:00 PM Monday through Thursday. It is normally finished by 11:00 PM.

Every night the NAS device is backed up to the Cloud Storage at XYZ Services. Because the weekly full only changes once a week, it really doesn't add any additional data to the daily backups. This backup is scheduled for 1:00 AM on Tuesday through Saturday. Daily jobs normally finish by 5:00 AM. The Weekend Full backup normally finishes Saturday evening.

Files are stored in the cloud storage as simple files and folders. So the backups are just really big files. This synchronization takes place at night and on weekends.

Obviously, your backup narrative will be different from this. But you get the idea.

At some point, we'll talk about the narrative for recovering files (and servers) in a disaster scenario. But, again, a competent technician will be able to figure that out from here.

If you still use tapes, or switch out RDX drives at clients, then you'll also need a sheet for the client to write down when they switched tapes/discs and which one they used. This is particularly important with RDX drives since most backup systems give all drives the same name and don't distinguish them electronically. So a good old label on the medium is the only way to know which one you want when it's time to restore.

Implementation Notes

Implementation here is pretty straight forward. you already have a backup strategy. After all, you've implemented something. Now you just need to write a few paragraphs about what you did.

Have your narrative reviewed by another technician and answer any questions they have. Chances are that a total stranger who wanders in to the office will have the same questions. Integrate these answers into your narrative.

The backup description (narrative) should live in the Network Documentation Binder onsite at the client's office. Since you will write it electronically, you can also save a copy on the client's server in the c:\!tech directory and on your own PSA system.

Depending on the client, you may want to go over this with them so they understand the backup process. Some clients really get into this stuff. But many clients will just have a blank stare. Don't force them to listen to you.

If you're not used to writing like this, don't fret. Chances are pretty good that you have YOUR way of doing things. As a result, most of your clients have pretty much the same backup system. So you can save a draft description of backup strategies and just tweak as needed for each client.

Remember The Two Great Weaknesses

- Backups that work
- Documentation

Just because you address the backup doesn't mean you can slack off on the documentation. Do both and you'll do your client a huge favor.

Recovery Test

It is extremely important that anyone who tries to help a client recover data understand the backup process. You can test this understanding very easily: Ask them to describe the restore points that exist right now.

The answer will look something like this:

- VSS from noon today
- Disc backup 11pm last night
- Disc from 2 days ago
- Cloud backup from last weekend

Every backup is different. They can be very similar, but they are each unique. Never get lazy. Never stop focusing on understanding your client backups. Never "Set it and forget it."

Three Take-Aways from This Chapter:

1. Start by creating a narrative description of your own backup.

2. Create backup documentation for each client. Save it in paper format and electronically.

3. Determine how you will remember to update this documentation when you make changes to a client's backup process.

Three Action Steps for Your Company:

1. _____

   _____

2. _____

   _____

3. _____

   _____

30

Backup Philosophies and Client Communication

The Ten Core Truths About Computer Backups

You really need a philosophy about how you talk about backups, and how you communicate with clients about them. As you can imagine, I encourage you to have a standard philosophy with all of your clients. Oddly enough, if a client has a strong alternative philosophy, *That's Good*! Most clients sort of vaguely know that they should have a backup. But they can't really articulate why, or what a good backup looks like.

What is a philosophy about backups? Quite simply, it's a standard set of beliefs or approaches you take. Here are the Ten Core Truths from our backup philosophy (Note: You might not like them all.):

Truth #1: Backup is not a disaster recovery plan

A good backup is one component in a DRP (disaster recovery plan), but it is not a DRP. It is necessary but not sufficient for a DRP. Therefore, it is more important than a DRP.

Truth #2: We build all backup systems with Disaster Recovery in mind

This goal keeps us focused on creating robust backup systems.

Truth #3: Good backup technologies don't fail on a regular basis; lazy clients and untrained technicians fail

Whenever we look at a technology developed by the "big boy" companies and used widely across the globe, we know that technology is solid. Tape backups, for example, are absolutely the most reliable backup. They fail because hardware is set up wrong, software is configured wrong, technicians don't know how to use the systems they're selling, or human beings fail to switch the tapes.

Tape backups aren't perfect. They are expensive compared to current hard drive technology, and they are slow. But if I drop a ten year old tape off the top of the Empire State Building into a puddle of mud, I'm going to be able to recover 100% of the data. That's not true with a hard drive.

Don't get me wrong: We're moving away from tape. But it's not because tape doesn't work. It's due to speed and price. We know we are moving to less reliable technologies (given that tape is the most reliable). Therefore, we have to be even more careful about the backup systems we create.

Truth #4: You (the technician) must absolutely master the backup technologies you sell and use

That means at the hardware level, software level, media level, and the process level. This is one of your muscles of success. You need to exercise it and build up muscle memory so that you make good decisions in a crisis and have a good sense of the resources available to you.

Truth #5: Backup media must be rotated to permanent offsite storage for several reasons

Permanent offsite storage means that they never come back. They sit on a shelf or in a vault essentially forever. Why?

a) Backups make a great snapshot in time for legal, financial, and H.R. reasons.

b) Each medium should only be used a certain number of times. If they are used continuously forever, the media become less reliable. This is true of tapes and hard drives equally. So that's why we take them out of circulation.

c) Backups go off site in case the office systems need to be recovered in a disaster. This might include a fire, water damage, or another event that makes it impossible to get to the office.

d) The goal of backups – including monthly off site backups – is to provide the ability to restore the client systems and data. Our normal preparation is for today, yesterday, and the last week. But it is also important sometimes to go back in time a month or two, or even a year or two.

There are no limits to the good reasons for storing media off site long-term. Theft, fire, flood, and all kinds of things can happen to your office. If they happen to your home or offsite storage facility on the same day, then you need to have a good business insurance (and maybe a good lawyer). How can you plan for that?

Truth #6: You should have as many "points in time" as feasible

This is critical. A basic backup will get you the file you deleted yesterday. A good backup will get you a file from last week or last month. A great backup will get you a file from several months or years back. A perfect backup will get your every version of every file ever created. (That perfect backup hasn't been invented yet, but it's good to think about.)

More than most technologies we deal with, backup systems have a very clear cost-quality relationship. You want something that kinda works? That's cheap. The perfect example is the USB drive brought home from Office Depot for $49. You plug it in and use whatever software is included. You kinda sorta think you can recover a file if needed. But if you can't access that software . . . um . . .?

At the other end of the scale are systems that cost millions of dollars and are the key components of zero-downtime, instant fail-over systems. In the middle, and much closer to the low end, are the $1,000-$2,000 systems we tend to put into client offices. From there you can move up to BDRs and cloud backups.

Create a simple checklist for your backup systems. Which points in time do you need to recover? Select (Yes) or (No) for each:

- One hour ago
- 12 hours ago
- Yesterday
- Three days ago
- Last week
- Two weeks ago
- Last Month
- Last Quarter
- 6 months back
- End of last year
- 12 months back
- 24 months back
- 5 years back
- 10 years back
- Other ?

Now consider what your media rotation looks like. What must it look like in order to create the restore points you say you want? Now think about #4 above: You must absolutely master the backup technologies you use. Let's say you're backing up to disc. After three months of backups, what exactly is on each of your backup discs? Are they full images? Copies of files? Versions of files? How many restore points do you have?

(Note: In Chapter Thirty-Two we'll talk about hard drive media and other technologies, their pros and cons.)

If your backup system does you the favor of eliminating duplicate files, does that mean file names or file versions? How exactly does it work? If you have bad sectors on your hard drive, have you lost every version of a specific file? Don't assume you know the answer. Master the technology.

Note: Many cloud backup systems fail horribly when it comes to restore points. Before you spend your money, learn what really goes on up in that cloud. Verify for yourself. Master the technology. If the only thing you can restore is the latest version of each file, is that good enough?

Truth #7: Use enough media to guarantee the restore points you want

Ideally, we would like to see at least 6-12 long-term storage media off site in addition to media for the current week. If you have a safe place to store the older media onsite, you could bring them back to the office.

Let's say you backup every business day. That's five times a week. Ideally, those are all full backups (we haven't used incremental backups since we moved away from reel-to-reel backups in 1995). So we have five "current" backups off site, plus end-of-month backups permanently off site for the last 12 months. That's a total of 17 media off site. If you have end-of-year backups, then you will have additional media off site.

Remember: The driver of this discussion is the number of restore points you need. Yes, it costs money. It's cheaper than going out of business.

Truth #8: The first media will fail

This philosophy is true far more often than we'd like to believe. Basically, it amounts to this: Assume that whatever media you use to restore from will be bad. The first hard drive, the first tape, the first cloud backup. Assume something will go wrong.

Clients don't change tapes/discs. Power supplies go out. Discs get corrupted. Databases get corrupted and then backed up. You need to restore from way back before the corruption happened.

Once you assume that you need backup plans for your backups, then you begin to plan at a higher level. Set up the Department of Redundancy Department within your office. Plan for failure; then plan around it. This is your job.

Truth #9: If you don't test your backup, you don't have a backup. If you can't restore from backup, you don't have a backup.

These are together because they're really the same thing. In addition to designing an awesome backup system, you need to design a process for restoring and testing that backup.

You don't need to perform a full restore in order to feel good about your backup. But you do need to restore from each drive that was backed up (e.g., C:, D:, x:), from each medium used (e.g., disc 1, disc

2), from the core O.S. area (system state on Windows machines), and from within key databases (e.g., a few mails within the Exchange database).

That's not trivial. Just like the backup, you need to craft a test restore that verifies you can get the data back where it belongs. This keeps your technicians tuned up on the process and verifies that you don't have hardware or software failures.

We recommend a test restore every month. If you can't do it remotely, plan to go onsite.

Truth #10: We can't care more about the client's backup than they do

Really, we do care more. But we have to tell ourselves that there's only so much we can do. If the client won't buy new media, won't take backups off site, won't let us get in to test restores . . . well, that's their choice. They get to decide how to spend their money. If they want the office manager to back up the data for a $12 MM company onto DVDs once a month, that's their decision.

We need to try to communicate to our clients, their employees, and our own employees about the importance of backups. We need to check them daily. And we need to push the client to take them seriously. But if they simply refuse to participate in the protection of their network, there's not much we can do.

On rare occasions, we have sent a memo to clients saying that we cannot be responsible for the success of their backups because they are not doing the things we outlined. We offer to do those things for them (including change backup devices every day) for a price. Sometimes it works, sometimes not. But when clients just don't care, we have to try not to worry about it.

Client Communications

When you discuss all this with clients, you need to step back from the geek-speak quite a bit. At the same time, you need to thoroughly understand your company philosophy and make sure the client understands.

We get push-back on taking tapes out of circulation from some folks. We get lots of resistance to switching media (tapes or discs). Interestingly enough, we rarely get resistance based on overall price.

It is extremely helpful to have stories you can use to illustrate your points. Collect backup stories. Believe me, I have one or more for every point above. Stories help them connect your philosophy with the world that matters to them.

Remember, most clients see backups as a necessary evil. It costs money but has few tangible rewards 99% of the time. Of course on the day you recover a database from six months ago, it is worthwhile. When the office burns down, a back is worthwhile. When an employee sabotages a system, a backup is worthwhile.

I highly recommend that you write up a one-page memo on your backup philosophy and distribute it to clients and prospects. It might all be "background noise" to most, but it is a real selling point – especially if you emphasize competence. Clients really want a good reason to justify the money they spend with you. Put yourself up against a $60/hr trunk slammer when it comes to backups.

It also helps to get client endorsements. I've got a great one from my long-time client Hank: "Karl saved my business twice in one year!" That kind of stuff goes a long ways.

Also, here's a great video: *How Pixar Almost Lost Toy Story 2* – at http://www.tested.com/videos/44220-how-pixar-almost-lost-toy-story-2-to-a-bad-backup.

That's the story about how Pixar lost the Toy Story 2 movie due to bad backups. Pixar. Bad backups for a MONTH. The lesson is: If it can happen to them, it can happen to you.

Take this seriously. Create a philosophy about backups that gives your clients rock solid backup plans that work.

Your To-Do List

First, you need to write out your philosophy about backups. Believe me: Most of your competition has NO philosophy about this critical function. AND almost no one who reads this will actually follow through either.

Use my discussion above as a starting place, but really make it your own. What do YOU like to see with regard to processes, procedures, off site media, etc.?

Second, you need to go over this with your technicians and make sure they all understand it. This might lead to some discussions or debate. That's fine: It means they're thinking about backups!

Third, you need to implement whatever pieces you do not currently have in place. This might include selling clients additional media in order to make sure they're in compliance with your philosophy.

Fourth, you need to communicate this to clients in some form (as discussed above). Handouts are good. The more professional looking the better.

Fifth, everyone on your team needs to support one another around this policy.

Three Take-Aways from This Chapter:

1. You have a backup philosophy – and SOPs. Write them down. Articulate them. Share them.

2. Having a thorough, consistent philosophy about backups can differentiate your company from the competition!

3. If you find yourself resisting this advice, it's worth thinking about why that is. At some level this is very complicated if you do it right. Take time and do it.

Three Action Steps for Your Company:

1. _____

   _____

2. _____

   _____

3. _____

   _____

31

Backup Monitoring, Testing, and Management

In the last few chapters we set up some backups, defined them, documented them, and spelled philosophies about backup and recovery. Now let's look at daily operations. When you manage the backups for several companies, you should have a systematic way of keeping track of what's going on – and documenting it.

Monitoring backups can be totally manual, totally automatic, or somewhere in the middle. I strongly favor somewhere in the middle. A totally manual backup monitoring means that you either sit down at the server or connect remotely and verify that the job ran, job finished, and job was successful. This is a very old-school way of doing things.

Totally automatic monitoring means that you trust some system to verify that a job started, job finished, and job finished *successfully*. This sounds like the super-cool future we all want. But it's very dangerous. In the last chapter I mentioned How Pixar Almost Lost Toy Story 2. That was possible because they had a super-cool automated backup system . . . that failed for a month and no one noticed.

Backups (and restores) are absolutely critical and therefore need more attention than that. Good enough isn't.

We highly recommend that you use a professional backup solution such as Backup Exec, which has rich reporting. We have never relied on the backup system built into Windows Server, but you could use that. Just make sure that you check those backups! If you're running SBS, you can get reports on backups via the built-in backup but not other solutions. Other solutions need to provide their own reporting.

If you have an RMM (remote monitoring and management) tool, you should find a backup that integrates with that tool so you can monitor backups automatically and remotely. As strange as it sounds, you will get false positive and false negative reports from all these tools. Backups will report a failure because they couldn't open a temporary file that just happened to be in use when the backup occurred but is unimportant and has since been removed by the system. Grrrr. And backups will report success even when they don't finish. Happily, this is rare.

The bottom line is: You need to actively monitor these systems. In truth, a well-designed backup system with good hardware and good software will work very well. Human error is the culprit 99% of the time when there's a failed backup. So you're monitoring your clients as well as their systems.

Create an automated system, but check it regularly. Trust but verify. I recommend the process defined in Chapter Thirteen: *Daily Monitoring of Client Machines*.

We certainly do not do a test restore every day, but we DO schedule a test restore every month along with monthly maintenance. As mentioned before, we restore the system state, something from each drive that was backed up (e.g., C:, D:, x:), something from each medium used (e.g., disc 1, disc 2), and from within key databases (e.g., a few mails within the Exchange database).

This takes time. And it may mean that you're onsite to perform these tasks. It's good for the client to see you doing some work rather than being 100% remote. It's also good for them to see you when it's not an emergency. It breaks them of the habit of saying "Oh no" every time you walk in the door.

The Big Picture

Your overall management of backups is arguably the most important thing your company does. It is the one thing that is guaranteed to keep your clients in business when disaster strikes. Maintenance is critical, but backups are more critical. Clients don't always see the importance here, but they will assume you're taking care of it when something goes bad.

In the big picture, managing backups is really a big sub-system of your managed service operation. That's why you need an overall philosophy that can be applied across all your clients. That's why you need standardized processes and procedures. That's why you need to train all of your staff to understand your philosophies and how they're implemented. That's why you do regular daily monitoring and monthly restores.

If you have enough clients, you might actually have one or two technicians who specialize in monitoring and managing client backups.

I know it's easy to put this off. After all, the backup does seem to work most of the time and other things break. But you have to keep in mind that the backup is more important than almost anything else. So spending a few minutes (per client) per day is a great investment of your time. Remember, one of my mantras is

Slow Down, Get More Done

This is a great example of that. A few minutes spent on backups every day can save many hours and dollars when something goes wrong down the road.

It is important to create a simple checklist, as we discussed in Chapter Thirty. Again, every technician needs to see this, touch it, and understand how critical it is to managing the client systems.

Three Take-Aways from This Chapter:

1. Determine how "automated" you want your backup monitoring to be. What is just the right level for you?

2. Similarly, how often will you restore data? Is this a monthly activity? Quarterly? More frequently? Less frequently?

3. If you have not been doing regular restores, start immediately. Make it a "Monthly Single" (see Chapter Twenty-Five). Determine how many are not working. You don't have to tell anyone. Just fix them.

Three Action Steps for Your Company:

1. _____

    _____

2. _____

    _____

3. _____

    _____

32

Changing Technologies for Backups

I am pretty bad at trivia. But once in a while I come through. One night our company had a Game Night at the office and we played *Trivia Pursuit 90's Edition*. I got a question about a technology that combines magnetic and optical technologies to store data. I stunned the crowd with the answer: **Floptical**.

In case you don't remember Floptical technology (see www.yesterdaystechnology.com/html/floptical_disks.html), it was like a floppy, but stored an amazing 21 MB of data on a single disc. Holy smokes, Batman! Slap in a SCSI card and with only an hour's worth of configuration, you've got a fast, fat backup!

But Floptical technology was replaced in the mid-90's with Zip Disks. Zip Disks could hold 100 Mb of data. That meant you only needed TEN discs to hold a Gigabyte. In fact, they used to sell a ten-pack

USED Iomega USB 100 Zip Drive and 11 - 100 MB disks
excellent working condition
Returns: Not accepted

Top-rated seller   2 bids   **$26.00**   11h 34m called a Giga-Pack. The ad shown here is from an eBay auction. It's over now, but don't fear! There are other Zip Disk auctions going on right now, so you can still get yours.

As you can imagine, it was not uncommon for people to use these technologies to back up their data. In fact, I knew someone whose job included two hours a day of swapping Floptical discs to back up a software development machine. Again: Not uncommon.

Old technology is not uncommon. After all, we're in an industry that changes at a dizzying pace. Many people run to whatever's new. New monitors, new processors, new memory, new storage. But when it comes to backup, you need to be very careful.

As you've seen in the last several chapters, we back up data for several reasons. Simple backups help us recover the file that disappeared yesterday. Better backups help us recover the files deleted six months ago. Thorough, well documented backups are the basis for a Disaster Recovery Plan. So think about it: Why do you do backups?

The answer to your "Why" question will help you pick the right backup medium.

Backup Media Limitations

Every medium has limitations. And all of the limitations are intertwined with one another. The primary limitations are:

- Capacity
- Speed
- Media lifetime
- Form factor lifetime
- Cost
- Ease of use
- Custody and access to media

Capacity speaks for itself. If you have a medium that stores 10Mb of data, you better be backing up a 386 computer with a 20 Mb hard drive! In the world of "big data," we don't expect a backup to fit on one disc or one tape. But in small business, the ideal is that a full backup *will* fit on one medium. When a backup starts going to a second tape or disc, you see failed and incomplete backups increase dramatically. That's because the user doesn't swap media. As simple as it is to change discs, you have exceeded the ease of use requirement for the client.

Speed is another obvious variable. If a backup does not finish by 8:00 AM, it probably interferes with business operations. So you need a medium that will hold a full backup and you need the speed to complete that backup within the window allowed. Many of us kick off backups at 10 PM or 11 PM. When backups go long, we can start them earlier. But with small business, we find lots of owners and managers logged on at nine o'clock at night, so our window is pretty limited.

Media lifetime refers to the time span in which you can safely retrieve all data before the media begin to degrade. For example, a cheap CD-ROM will only last two years. A good CD-ROM written by a poor-quality device will only last ten. Archive quality media with high quality hardware will theoretically last 50 or 100 years. See www.audioholics.com/education/audio-formats-technology/cd-and-dvd-longevity-how-long-will-they-last.

But in the real world, many clients (and consultants) have used the cheapest media available and the cheapest hardware to write it with. How many? Maybe 90%? Maybe more? It's another example of the Paradox of Simplicity: I can create a CD. I can read it from another machine. Therefore, I have a good copy/backup.

Well, there's good and there's good enough. If that cheap CD written with that cheap CD burner lasts five years, is that **good enough**?

Form factor lifetime refers to the time period when you can expect to find the specific media and related hardware/software available for use in restoring data. Floptical technology had a very short lifespan. Zip disks had a longer lifespan, but are nonetheless hard to find today. Reel to reel tape may be perfectly capable of recovery, but you still need a tape player! DDS and various kinds of DLT/SLT tapes have enjoyed a very long lifetime. The key to their success has been a commitment to reading older tapes. A DDS5 drive will read a DDS4 tape even if it can't write to it.

Cost is partially self-explanatory. There's the obvious cost of buying the hardware, software, and media. Then there are the hidden costs of operation and recovery. How much labor does it take to manage backups regularly? Note that reliability will have a significant effect on this. A less reliable system will require more labor . . . and probably be more expensive in the long run. The cost of recovering data could also be significant, especially if pieces of the system are obsolete.

Ease of use is critical to success. Of course you need to be able to configure, monitor, and test backups. Likewise, you need to be able to restore data and entire systems as needed. When technology is new this is much easier than when it gets old. Restoring from old or obsolete backup systems can be extremely time consuming and expensive. And, most importantly, you have to be very careful not to damage the backup at any time.

Remember Truth #4 from the *Ten Core Truths About Computer Backups* (Chapter Thirty): **You must absolutely master the backup technologies you sell and use.** When you stumble across older technologies, you will need to come up to speed before you start messing with media. That involves one of the great rules of success: Slow down, get more done.

If you start a sloppy recovery, you might end up repeating work, starting over, and wasting a lot of time. If you do something wrong, you might destroy backup data and mess up the recovery altogether. Systems that are easy to use are not necessarily lower quality or less effective. The easier a system is to use, the more effective it will be in the long run. Of course, all of these things are relative. You need to balance the variables.

Custody and access to media have generally not been an important concern until remote backups and cloud services became popular. After all, whether you're backing up to Floptical discs, tapes, or hard drives, you maintain custody at all times or your backups are moved to and from a secure offsite storage facility by a bonded agent. It's really only with cloud-based backups that we lose control of our data. If your data storage company violates your company or industry standards, moves a copy of your data out of the country, or simply doesn't document where your data are stored, you have no control over that. You may never know these things are happening.

And when something goes wrong, you may have no recourse. I believe the horror stories on this point will continue to grow. The laws governing this technology are made by legislators who can't set up an external USB drive and disputes are settled by judges who have their emails printed out by secretaries and placed in their in-box each morning. Talk about the wild west! The point here is that Cloud Backups may be the ultimate backup in terms of flexibility, reliability, timeliness, etc. – but you have to address the issues of custody and access to data more seriously than ever before.

If you manage clients who need to comply with HIPAA, SOX, or other legal requirements, you need to make sure that your cloud vendors document their processes and custody policies. Luckily, the good ones are pretty good at this.

Picking Media and Form Factors

In an ever-changing world, how do you decide which technology to invest in? To answer that question, you need to define the kind of backups and archiving you need. For many businesses, the longest you will ever have to worry about a financial audit is seven years. In some industries, you're required to keep records for ten, twenty, or more years. Some records need to be maintained for the lifetime of the patient. Some records need to be retained forever.

You need a process and technology to fit your needs.

If all of this data exists as "live" data in some format, then you can continually modify your backup systems, never letting the current system become obsolete. At some point, you might add an entire archive of data to the "live" data, thus guaranteeing that that archive will always be included in the current backup. That takes a lot of disc space and time, so you'll need to balance cost and time requirements.

More and more industries are requiring lengthy or permanent backups of specific data.

Just make sure that you are an informed adviser to your clients. Make sure they understand that all of this takes money. And then proceed to design, build, and maintain systems that are as reliable as needed for as long as needed. Again, you're balancing all of the factors discussed.

Cloud and Disc Backups

Tape is finally fading within small businesses due to cost and speed. And, to be honest, many technicians have never made the effort to master SCSI technology and tape backups (those used to be tied to one another). At this time, various kinds of disc-based backups are in play. Most of them are great for simple backups. But for longer-range backups, they are as expensive as tapes because the media need to be taken out of circulation.

Interestingly enough, most disc-based backup systems fail on several levels with regard to creating fast, reliable backups with significant restore points. They are easy to use, but not great at creating reliable backups or disaster recovery systems. Again, the Paradox of Simplicity. They're "good enough" for simple backups. But are they good enough for long-term archives and disaster recovery?

I am afraid, for many reasons, that this period of disc-based backups will become an era of failed recoveries. Fifteen years from now, technology schools will teach the lessons of poor backup designs and point to this time period for lots of examples. Luckily, like Floptical drives, this era appears to be short-lived.

I exclude from this discussion the well-designed disc-to-disc, disc-to-disc-to-tape, and disc-to-disc-to-cloud backup systems. Good systems of this kind tend to use SAN technology, redundant arrays, and high speed data lines. That necessarily puts them outside the budget constraints of most small businesses.

Cloud backups, or disc-to-disc-to-cloud backups, appear to be the answer to many of the most difficult challenges of reliable backups with multiple restore points. Cloud backups have virtually unlimited capacity. Some systems have virtually unlimited versioning. Point-in-time snapshots have been a weakness, but that has more to do with personal habits than technology. A few good lawsuits will bring that behavior back in line. Just give it time.

Speed is still a major concern for many cloud-based backup systems. But if you backup to disc onsite and then backup from disc to cloud, speed becomes less relevant because the disc-to-disc piece is fast and can be completed overnight and then the cloud component can trickle up as needed. You still have bandwidth considerations, so cost can still play a big role.

Is cloud backup the ultimate, perfect backup? No. It scores very well on many variables, but the variables are always a mix.

Cloud backup certainly has capacity. Media lifetime is kind of irrelevant since the cloud storage company takes on the responsibility of making your data available. They have to worry about media, form factor, and media lifetime issues on their end. Your job is to choose the right vendor so you can feel comfortable that these things are being taken care of!

Speed and cost are still significant variables. Microsoft seems to be betting the farm that Internet connectivity will be super-fast and super-cheap in order to make their plans work. But we're certainly not there yet. If you want simple file recovery, then there are many options. If you want versioning that goes back 12 months, you have fewer options and higher expenses. If you want true snapshots or images (not "snapshots" reconstructed from versions) then costs go way up and options are slim.

In all of this, ease of use can be very deceptive. It's the ultimate Paradox of Simplicity: Anyone can create a backup to the cloud that makes them feel good and safe but provides no real security for the data. It seems so simple. And if you have very little technical knowledge, all the systems seem good and reliable. As a result, people are placing the entire future security of their businesses on technology that is often inappropriate for their needs.

More than ever, businesses need good advisers to help them make the right decisions regarding backups. If that's you, please see Truth #4 again: You must absolutely master the backup technologies you sell and use. You need to have a philosophy about backups and disaster recovery. You need to have a "system" you prefer and sell. You need to train your team on YOUR way of building, maintaining, and testing backups.

You can't be lazy about this. Every single time you build and sell a new server or storage system, you need to build and document the backup and recovery strategy that works best for THIS client and THIS data.

Three Take-Aways from This Chapter:

1. Did I mention that you must absolutely master the backup technologies you sell and use?

2. It is always easier to master one technology than ten. If you can sell a consistently reliable, reasonably priced backup system to all of your clients, you increase the probability for good backups and reliable restores.

3. If you sell cloud backups, be very sure to verify that you can restore all the versions your clients might ever need.

Three Action Steps for Your Company:

1. _____

   _____

2. _____

   _____

3. _____

   _____

33

Disaster Recovery - Simple Restores

What is a disaster?

For a business, it's pretty much anything that causes a widespread stoppage of business. That might mean a server down, or Exchange down, or the company's commerce web site down. In this article we're going to look at a specific scenario.

Most small businesses only need to deal with three basic types of business interruption: 1) Utility outage (power outage, internet outage); 2) Server crash (some critical function on the primary server renders it unusable); or 3) building-wide disaster (fire, hazmat spill). A fourth, less likely scenario would be a region-wide disaster. This would include major floods, major hurricanes, major earthquakes, etc.

Please Note: When you create a disaster recovery procedure, it must exist as a set of written documents. Everyone in our business wants to put everything in an electronic format. Please don't argue with me on this. This is disaster preparedness, fergoodnessake. Let's say the emergency is a power outage. Or a failed hard disc. Or a fire. Or a flood. Or a hazmat spill that requires the neighborhood to be evacuated.

Get the picture? In an emergency of almost any kind, the kind that would require you to implement this plan, you won't have access to the plan in electronic format! It is totally fine to have the plan exist primarily in electronic format, but there should be a printed version for the day the lights are out and the water is rising.

What is a Simple Restore?

There are many kinds of disaster recovery. In the most complicated and expensive, the goal is to completely recreate the failed network in every detail. This doesn't work well in small businesses. If your old system had a three year old server and 50 machines ranging from Windows 7 to XP, you are very unlikely to recreate that environment exactly.

A second type of disaster recovery focuses on active directory. The goal is to bring back the server, with all the data and all of the network SIDs for machines and users. It does not require the exact hardware that existed before, but focuses on the most important pieces of the network, which could easily be on new hardware.

The third most common type of disaster recovery involves simply "getting your data back." That includes total server recovery in some cases. Two examples of this are very common: Recovering from a failed hard drive and restoring an entire server from tape or disc. These are simple restores.

Rule #1: Go Slow!

Disaster recoveries are always stressful. No matter how good your system is or how often you've tested it, there's always a chance that something went wrong with the last backup. Or the backup software won't load.

And then there's human error. You might over-write newer data with older data. You might not write-protect a restore medium, and it might get written to as soon as your mount it because the next backup job is waiting for it. Stuff happens.

Think. Think. Think. Go slow. Be careful. Be methodical. Know what you know. And once you completely master the technology in front of you and the resources available to you, your chances of success go way up.

Rule #2: Make a Plan

Please do not show up, slap in a new hard drive and then start to think "What should I do first?" You've already done first. Or maybe you did second or third and skipped first altogether.

A plan – a checklist – is critical to success because it guarantees that you will do everything you need to do, and in the order you need to do it. It also makes sure you don't skip the "small" steps that make life easier in the long run. For example, we like to label hard drives before we put them in the system. This allows us to note exactly where they were as we take them out. No matter how much switching and swapping takes place, we can get the system back to where it was when we showed up on the scene.

You also want to mark the old (bad) hard drive. We take a large permanent marker and make a big X across the top of the drive. Then we write BAD and the date it was removed from service.

If you are using a cloud-based D.R. system, how do you notify them that you need to execute the D.R.? And how do you actually bring that data down to an empty hard drive? What's the plan? What's the checklist?

Rule #3: Use a TSR Log

and Document Everything You Do

A Troubleshooting and Repair log (See Volume Three, Chapter Thirty) should be started as soon as you begin logging time on the service request. You should make a note with each important action step you take, and you should make a note at least once every 15 minutes. The TSR log will help you document everything you do and will help you troubleshoot in case something goes wrong.

These three rules will give you a high level of success – and confidence in your process.

Simple restores are just was stressful as any other disaster recovery. They are "simple" only in the fact that you're doing two basic things: 1) Fix the system, and 2) Reload the data. But those two things can be rather big and troublesome on their own, so "simply" doing them might not be simple at all.

The other thing that's nice about simple restores is that you can hand them off to lesser-qualified technicians.

Gulp.

That's right. Once you have the checklist down, you can have it executed by anyone. This is a bit scary until you realize how good it makes YOU. You have to be crystal clear about making sure they understand the dangers and the basic process. They need to verify that a backup job is not waiting for a medium. They need to label all the drives, including the new one and the old one. They need to be able to identify the correct media to restore from.

When you can guide them through the pitfalls and pleasures of data restore while they're onsite and you are not, then you know you have a great checklist.

Rule #4: Improve Your Process

When you are finished with any "emergency" data recovery, you should take stock of what went wrong – or could have gone better. Did you know how to do a bare metal restore with this specific backup system? If a medium was bad, did you know the next best restore point, where it was located, and have it available?

Lots of people (myself included) preach that you do not have a backup until you test your restore. Similarly, you do not have a disaster recovery until you test your D.R. That means you have to learn each system you have in place well enough to actually execute a recovery. The time to learn this is before disaster strikes, not after.

So whatever needs improvement, make a note. Whatever you needed and didn't have on hand, make a note. Add all these notes to the TSR log and then use them to update the checklist. What's the last item on the checklist? "Update this checklist."

Hurricanes, floods, and fires are real. So are hard drive crashes. You need to know what you need to know before you need it!

Three Take-Aways from This Chapter:

1. You can prepare for the unexpected. This is especially true if you plan a simple restore.

2. Start with the Server-Build checklists you create for new servers, and fine-tune them for a generic "simple restore" recovery project.

3. Train technicians by restoring servers from your own backups to new hardware (use old machines you have lying around).

Three Action Steps for Your Company:

1. _____

   _____

2. _____

   _____

3. _____

   _____

34

One Final Note

It may seem hard to believe, but I have SO much more to write. I am grateful to get this four-book series out of my brain and onto paper. But I have many other projects left to tackle. For example, I still have hundreds of pages of checklists and documentation forms that sit on my server, waiting to be shared.

Stay tuned.

I started working on this project in May of 2011 – more than three years ago. My basic idea was this:

1) I already write a blog. I'll write my next book by blogging basic ideas for each chapter. Thus the SOP Friday blog posts were born on blog.smallbizthoughts.com.

2) I picked processes and procedures from my "\operations\ processes and procedures" folder on the server and started describing each of them.

3) I assembled a team of artists, graphics professionals, layout professionals, and proofreaders to build the books.

4) I raised money through the crowd-funding site Indiegogo.com to help pay for all that. This made it possible to speed up the work considerably.

5) I got to about the 90% mark on blogging the book in December of 2013. Then, in February of 2014 I put my head down and started turning hundreds of blog posts and documents into these four books.

6) This project has been my job about thirty hours a week for the last six month. And a few hours a week for the three years before that!

Today I set it free. There will be minor edits and graphics tweaking. I need to deal with the Library of Congress, the U.S. Copyright Office, printers, publishers, and distributors.

Please believe that this is absolutely and completely sincere:

> I love what I do and I love the SMB technology consulting community that makes it possible for me to do this. I love writing. I love speaking. I love traveling around and meeting everyone.

> Four years ago I transformed every single aspect of my life. And thanks to you – the SMB Community – I have created a world in which I can do this. I survive and thrive because of your support.

> You made it possible for me to take three years of my life to create this four-book set. As long as I live, I will be grateful to God and to you for making this happen.

> Go forth. Be successful. And email me if I can ever help with anything.

> Very sincerely,

> Karl W. Palachuk

> karlp@smallbizthoughts.com

Appendix A:
Definitions and Acronyms

BDR   Backup and Disaster Recovery. Normally refers to a devices that can help a client to get back into business very quickly (as opposed to a simple backup, which may take the client a long time to get back into business).

DDC   Disc to Disc to Cloud – a backup strategy.

DDT   Disc to Disc to Tape – a backup strategy.

CRM   Customer Relationship Management. A software package or hosted service that allows you to track all interactions with your clients. Some PSA systems have CRM modules.

HaaS   Hardware as a Service. A service in which the consultant owns the hardware and provides it to the client for a monthly service fee.

ILO   HP's Integrated Lights Out hardware. Allows a technician to connect to a server remotely at the hardware level.

IS   Information Systems. See also Information Technology.

IT   Information Technology. See also Information Systems.

LOB   Line of Business application. A type of software specific to a given industry (or line of business).

MMC   Monthly Maintenance Checklist

NDB   Network Documentation Binder

PSA   Professional Services Administration. A type of software that includes modules for running your professional service business.

RAID   Redundant Array of Independent Drives. A collection of drive configurations that provide a level of redundancy so that the server can continue to operate in case a hard drive fails.

RMM   Remote Monitoring and Management tool.

SBS   Small Business Server

Service Request   As used in this series, identical to Service Ticket.

Service Ticket   As used in this series, identical to Service Request.

SMB   Small and Medium Business

SOP   Standard Operating Procedures

SR   Service Request. As used in this series, identical to Service Ticket.

Appendix B:
Resources

Books and Articles

"CD and DVD Longevity: How Long Will they Last?" See www.audioholics.com/education/audio-formats-technology/cd-and-dvd-longevity-how-long-will-they-last.

The E-Myth Revisited by Michael E. Gerber

Floptical technology. See www.yesterdaystechnology.com/html/floptical_disks.html.

Network Documentation Workbook by Karl W. Palachuk. See www.networkdocumentationworkbook.com.

Project Management in Small Business by Dana J Goulston, PMP, and Karl W. Palachuk.

Service Agreements for SMB Consultants: A Quick-Start Guide to Managed Services by Karl W. Palachuk. See www.serviceagreementsforsmbconsultants.com.

"Impact on U.S. Small Business of Natural & Man-Made Disasters." A Report by HP and SCORE. See www.webwizebackup.com/impactofDisaster.pdf.

Software and Services

Adobe Acrobat. Tool for creating industry-standard PDF files. See www.adobe.com.

The ASCII Group. Membership organization for technology consultants and resellers. See www.ascii.com.

Autotask PSA. See www.autotask.com.

Backup Exec. Software made by Symantec. See www.symantec.com/products/data-backup-software.

ConnectWise PSA. See www.connectwise.com.

Continuum. Remote management and monitoring tool with an outsourced service for escalated tech support. See www.continuum.net.

Dove Help Desk. Outsourced service for escalated tech support. www.dovehelpdesk.com.

GFI Max. Remote management and monitoring tool/service. See www.gfimax.com.

LabTech. Remote management and monitoring tool/service. See www.labtechsoftware.com.

PDF Complete. Tool for creating industry-standard PDF files. See www.pdfcomplete.com.

Robocopy is a tool distributed primarily via the Microsoft Server Resource Kits since NT 3.5. http://technet.microsoft.com/en-us/library/cc733145.aspx.

Servers Alive. Great software for monitoring whether specific services are running across the Internet. See www.woodstone.nu/salive.

Third Tier. Outsourced service for escalated tech support. See
www.thirdtier.net.

TigerPaw PSA. See www.tigerpawsoftware.com.

Misc. Web Sites

How Pixar Almost Lost Toy Story 2 – at
http://www.tested.com/videos/44220-how-pixar-almost-lost-
toy-story-2-to-a-bad-backup

Other Resources from Small Biz Thoughts

Please Check Out Our Web Sites:

www.SMBBooks.com

This is our primary site for books on technical topics, managed services, running your business, and more. All of our up-coming training events and recorded programs are there as well.

www.SmallBizThoughts.com

blog.SmallBizThoughts.com

This is our primary web site and Karl's popular blog for I.T. Consultants and Managed Service Providers. You can also find out about SOPs (standard operating procedures) and business coaching through this web site.

Karl's Weekly Newsletter

Register at one of the sites above or at GreatLittleBook.com.

This newsletter covers upcoming events, seminars, news, and "what's happening" in the SMB Consulting space.

Please also consider these fine books by Great Little Book:

Managed Services in a Month 2nd ed.

Build a Successful IT Services Business in 30 Days.

by Karl W. Palachuk

2013

208 pages

A no-nonsense guide to building a successful managed service practice.

Whether you are just starting out, or converting your existing break/fix technology consulting business to managed services, this book will show you the way. The newly revised and expanded 2nd edition has nine new chapters, covering the latest products and services available today-including cloud technologies.

Also available as an e-book, audio book, or in a Spanish language translation.

The #1 book on Managed Services on Amazon.com for more than five years!

Service Agreements for SMB Consultants

A Quick-Start Guide to Managed Services

by Karl W. Palachuk

2006

185 pages

This great little book does a lot more than give you sample agreements.

Karl starts out with a discussion of how you run your business and the kinds of clients you want to have. The combination of these – defining yourself and defining your clients – is the basis for your service agreements.

Includes sample contracts with commentaries. All text, as well as some other great resources are provided as downloads.

Available in paperback or e-book formats.

www.SMBBooks.com

www.SmallBizThoughts.com

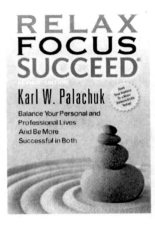

Relax Focus Succeed®

Balance Your Personal and Professional Lives and Be More Successful in Both

by Karl W. Palachuk

2013

296 pages

The premise of this book is simple but powerful: The fundamental keys to success are focus, hard work, and balance. Too often, the advice we receive gives plenty of attention to focus and hard work, but very little to balance.

This great little book will help you believe that you need balance, show you the power of focus, and help you move forward with the new you -- a happier, healthier, better balanced, and more successful you.

www.SMBBooks.com

www.SmallBizThoughts.com

Calling all SMB IT Professionals!

The ChannelPro Network is dedicated to providing IT consultants, VARs and MSPs the news, insights, resources and best practices necessary to help them grow their businesses and better serve their SMB customers.

Sign up for free today
Website | Live Events | Monthly Magazine

ChannelPro

ChannelProNetwork.com

CPSIA information can be obtained at www.ICGtesting.com
Printed in the USA
BVOW03s1321260914

368401BV00009B/47/P